VILLERS
BOCAGE

The 'Battle Zone Normandy' Series

All of these titles can be ordered via the
Sutton Publishing website
www.suttonpublishing.co.uk

The 'Battle Zone Normandy'
Editorial and Design Team

Series Editor Simon Trew

Senior Commissioning Editor Jonathan Falconer

Assistant Editor Nick Reynolds

Cover and Page Design Martin Latham

Editing and Layout Donald Sommerville

Mapping Map Creation Ltd

Photograph Scanning and Mapping Bow Watkinson

Index Michael Forder

BATTLE ZONE NORMANDY

VILLERS BOCAGE

GEORGE FORTY

Series Editor: Simon Trew

Foreword: Viscount Montgomery of Alamein

Sutton Publishing

First Published in 2004 by
Sutton Publishing Limited · Phoenix Mill
Thrupp · Stroud · Gloucestershire · GL5 2BU

Text Copyright © George Forty 2004
Tour map overlays Copyright © Sutton
Publishing
Tour base maps Copyright © Institut
Géographique National, Paris
GSGS (1944) map overlays Copyright ©
Sutton Publishing
GSGS (1944) base maps Copyright ©
The British Library/Crown Copyright

British Library Cataloguing in Publication Data
A catalogue record for this book is available
from The British Library.

ISBN 0-7509-3012-8

While every effort has been made to ensure
that the information given in this book is
accurate, the publishers, the author and the
series editor do not accept responsibility for
any errors or omissions or for any changes in
the details given in this guide or for the
consequence of any reliance on the
information provided. The publishers would be
grateful if readers would advise them of any
inaccuracies they may encounter so these can
be considered for future editions of this book.
The inclusion of any place to stay, place to eat,
tourist attraction or other establishment in
this book does not imply an endorsement or
recommendation by the publisher, the series
editor or the author. Their details are included
for information only. Directions are for
guidance only and should be used in
conjunction with other sources of information.

Typeset in 10.5/14 pt Sabon

Printed and bound in England by
J.H. Haynes & Co. Ltd, Sparkford

Front cover: Stuart V of 7th Armoured Division somewhere in the *bocage* on 15 June 1944.
(Imperial War Museum [IWM] B5608)

Page 1: The Place du Dorset Regiment in Hottot-les-Bagues and the memorial to 231st Infantry
Brigade. *(Author)*

Page 3: Sherman OP knocked out in Villers-Bocage by *SS-Obersturmführer* Michael Wittmann of
2nd Company, 101st Heavy SS Panzer Battalion. *(Bundesarchiv 101/1738/267/28a)*

Page 7: Wittmann's Tiger tank *en route* to Normandy. *(Bundesarchiv 101/299/1804/7)*

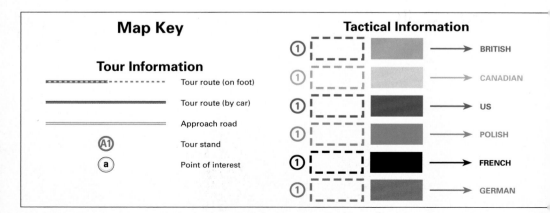

Map Key

Tour Information

- Tour route (on foot)
- Tour route (by car)
- Approach road
- (A1) Tour stand
- (a) Point of interest

Tactical Information

- BRITISH
- CANADIAN
- US
- POLISH
- FRENCH
- GERMAN

CONTENTS

THE NORMANDY BATTLEFIELD

Legend	
●	Town
——	Railway
——	Road
⊥⊥⊥⊥	Caen Canal
– – –	Département boundary

Contour 100 metres
Contour 200 metres
Contour 300 metres

0   25   50
Kilometres

Bay of the Seine

Cherbourg

Valognes   Quineville
Montebourg
Ste. Mère Eglise   UTAH
Barneville
R. Douve   OMAHA   Port en Bessin   Arromanches   Courseulles   Le Havre
St. Laurent   GOLD   JUNO
Carentan   Isigny   R. Aure   SWORD   Cabourg
Bayeux   Ouistreham   Houlgate
Lessay   R. Taute   Caen   Argences   Lisieu
Périers   R. Drôme   R. Seulles   R. Odon
MANCHE   St. Lô   Caumont   Mézidon
Coutances   R. Vire   Villers-Bocage
CALVADOS   R. Dives
Granville   R. Orne   Falaise
Condé   R. Orne   Argentan
Vire   Flers
Avranches   ORNE
Mortain   Domfront
R. Sélune   R. Mayenne   Alençon
Fougères

PART ONE

INTRODUCTION

BATTLE ZONE NORMANDY

The Battle of Normandy was one of the greatest military clashes of all time. From late 1943, when the Allies appointed their senior commanders and began the air operations that were such a vital preliminary to the invasion, until the end of August 1944, it pitted against one another several of the most powerful nations on earth, as well as some of their most brilliant minds. When it was won, it changed the world forever. The price was high, but for anybody who values the principles of freedom and democracy, it is difficult to conclude that it was one not worth paying.

I first visited Lower Normandy in 1994, a year after I joined the War Studies Department at the Royal Military Academy Sandhurst (RMAS). With the 50th anniversary of D-Day looming, it was decided that the British Army would be represented at several major ceremonies by one of the RMAS's officer cadet companies. It was also suggested that the cadets should visit some of the battlefields, not least to bring home to them the significance of why they were there. Thus, at the start of June 1994, I found myself as one of a small team of military and civilian directing staff flying with the cadets in a draughty and noisy Hercules transport to visit the beaches and fields of Calvados, in my case for the first time.

I was hooked. Having met some of the veterans and seen the ground over which they fought – and where many of their friends died – I was determined to go back. Fortunately, the Army encourages battlefield touring as part of its soldiers' education, and on numerous occasions since 1994 I have been privileged to return to Normandy, often to visit new sites. In the process I have learned a vast amount, both from my colleagues (several of whom are contributors to this series) and from my enthusiastic and sometimes tri-service audiences, whose professional insights and penetrating questions have frequently made me re-examine my own assumptions and prejudices. Perhaps inevitably, especially when standing in one of Normandy's beautifully-maintained Commonwealth War Graves Commission cemeteries, I have also found myself deeply moved by the critical events that took place there in the summer of 1944.

'Battle Zone Normandy' was conceived by Jonathan Falconer, Commissioning Editor at Sutton Publishing, in 2001. Why not, he suggested, bring together recent academic research – some of which challenges the general perception of what happened on and after 6 June 1944 – with a perspective based on familiarity with the ground itself? We agreed that the opportunity existed for a series that would set out to combine detailed and accurate narratives, based mostly on primary sources, with illustrated guides to the ground itself, which could be used either in the field (sometimes quite literally), or by the armchair explorer. The book in your hands is the product of that agreement.

The 'Battle Zone Normandy' series consists of 14 volumes, covering most of the major and many of the minor engagements that went together to create the Battle of Normandy. The first six books deal with the airborne and amphibious landings on 6 June 1944, and with the struggle to create the firm lodgement that was the prerequisite for eventual Allied victory. Five further volumes cover some of the critical battles that followed, as the Allies' plans unravelled and they were forced to improvise a battle very different from that originally intended. Finally, the last three titles in the series examine the fruits of the bitter attritional struggle of June and July 1944, as the Allies irrupted through the German lines or drove them back in fierce fighting. The series ends, logically enough, with the devastation of the German armed forces in the 'Falaise Pocket' in late August.

Whether you use these books while visiting Normandy, or to experience the battlefields vicariously, we hope you will find them as interesting to read as we did to research and write. Far from the inevitable victory that is sometimes represented, D-Day and the ensuing battles were full of hazards and unpredictability. Contrary to the view often expressed, had the invasion failed, it is far from certain that a second attempt could have been mounted. Remember this, and the significance of the contents of this book, not least for your life today, will be the more obvious.

Dr Simon Trew
Royal Military Academy Sandhurst
December 2003

INTRODUCTION

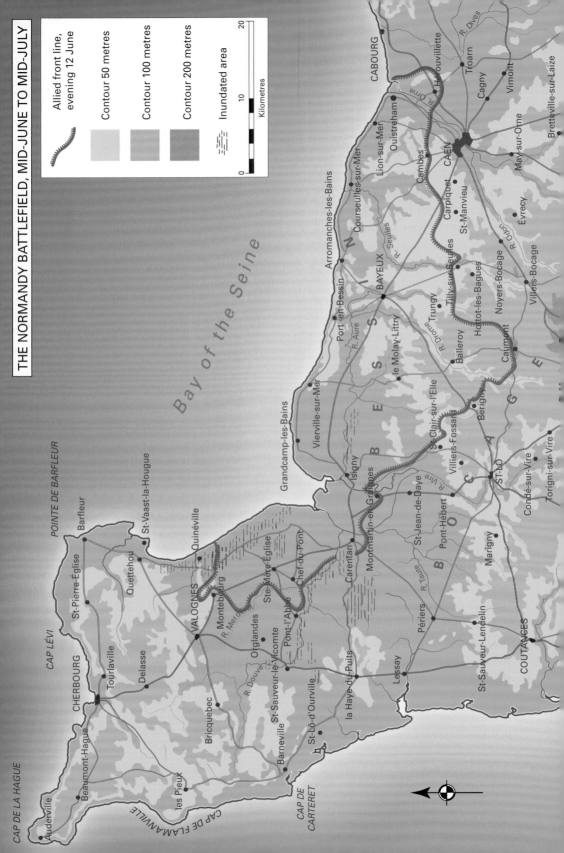

THE NORMANDY BATTLEFIELD, MID-JUNE TO MID-JULY

Allied front line, evening 12 June

Contour 50 metres

Contour 100 metres

Contour 200 metres

Inundated area

Kilometres

0   10   20

Bay of the Seine

POINTE DE BARFLEUR

CAP LÉVI

CAP DE LA HAGUE

CAP DE FLAMANVILLE

CAP DE CARTERET

Auderville
Beaumont-Hague
CHERBOURG
St-Pierre-Église
Barfleur
St-Vaast-la-Hougue
Quinéville
Tourlaville
Quettehou
Delasse
VALOGNES
Montebourg
Ste-Mère-Église
Chef-du-Pont
Pont-l'Abbé
Orglandes
Bricquebec
St-Sauveur-le-Vicomte
les Pieux
Barneville
St-Lô-d'Ourville
la Haye-du-Puits
Carentan
Lessay
Périers
St-Sauveur-Lendelin
COUTANCES
Montmartin-en-Graignes
St-Jean-de-Daye
Pont-Hébert
Marigny
ST-LÔ
Condé-sur-Vire
Torigni-sur-Vire
Villiers-Fossard
Bérigny
St-Clair-sur-l'Elle
Isigny
Vierville-sur-Mer
Grandcamp-les-Bains
Port-en-Bessin
Arromanches-les-Bains
Courseulles-sur-Mer
Lion-sur-Mer
Ouistreham
CABOURG
Tro.arn
Hérouvillette
CAEN
Cambes
Carpiquet
St-Manvieu
St-Mauvieu
Cagny
Vimont
May-sur-Orne
Bretteville-sur-Laize
Évrecy
Villers-Bocage
Noyers-Bocage
Hottot-les-Bagues
Tilly-sur-Seulles
Trungy
Balleroy
Caumont
BAYEUX
le Molay-Littry

R. Dives
R. Orne
R. Odon
R. Seulles
R. Aure
R. Drôme
R. Elle
R. Vire
R. Taute
R. Douve
R. Merderet

Bay of the Seine

BESSIN
BOCAGE

FOREWORD

The invasion of Normandy in June 1944 was the largest single operation in the history of warfare. It initiated the last phase of the Second World War, which culminated in the unconditional surrender of all German forces in May 1945. It was a masterpiece of planning, coordination, leadership and dedication to duty, a high point in Anglo-American cooperation.

Rommel was the German battlefield commander, and an established adversary of Monty, his British counterpart and Allied Land Forces Commander until the successful conclusion of the Battle of Normandy in August 1944. By then it was clear that the Allies would win the war. The establishment of the bridgehead in the aftermath of D-Day was vital, but it then required some very tough fighting to create the conditions for the breakout.

In this context the operations around Villers-Bocage, where the renowned 7th Armoured Division suffered a serious setback, provide a fascinating study. That area of Normandy, so beautiful in early summer, was extremely difficult terrain for armoured warfare against an implacable foe with superior armaments. The temporary reverse at Villers-Bocage also caused difficulties in the otherwise most harmonious Anglo-American alliance. The reader will discover, while following this new and admirable guide, just how difficult it was, and why the troops deployed in the area deserve high praise for their courage and determination.

George Forty was commissioned in 1948 and joined the 1st Royal Tank Regiment in Germany; thus we overlapped in the same regiment for the last few months of my military service. After a distinguished career he retired and became the Director of the Tank Museum at Bovington. Author of many books, George is amply qualified to write this guide so that succeeding generations may study the battles that enabled Europe to be at peace with itself for 60 years.

Viscount Montgomery of Alamein, CMG, CBE
London, August 2003

AUTHOR'S INTRODUCTION

Very seldom do events on the battlefield go 'according to plan'. There are so many factors to be considered, some of which, like the prevailing weather conditions or the topography, are virtually outside the control of the planners, that the organising of battles is not an exact science. Often some factor that seemed at first sight to be almost irrelevant and not worthy of much attention suddenly assumes enormous importance. When a number of such factors come together unexpectedly, then the planners can find themselves in real trouble. This was the case at the start of the 'enlargement of the beachhead' phase of Operation 'Overlord'. The initial invasion had gone, on the whole, spectacularly well. The Allies had secured a firm toehold in Normandy, while the Germans were still confused as to whether this was the main assault or merely a feint, many of their senior generals still favouring the Pas de Calais as the real point of attack for the main invasion. Also, while their troops on the ground fought bravely enough, it was becoming more and more difficult for them to move up their reserves, in particular their all-important panzer divisions, principally because of the wide-ranging superiority of Allied air power. Nevertheless, the planned-for gains anticipated on D-Day had not all been achieved, and now it was vital to link up the beachheads, get more troops, their weapons and equipment ashore, and start to push further inland.

In the British/Canadian sector, the important city of Caen (a D-Day objective) had not yet been taken; nevertheless, the leading troops were already off the beaches, the front line was on average some ten kilometres inland and there was much cause for optimism. A week later, however, the anticipated progress had still not been made and there even seemed to be a chance that operations might grind to a halt, some talk even being about a return to the stalemate trench warfare of the First World War. Of course it can be argued that this had all been anticipated and was just part of the overall Allied plan, namely that the British and

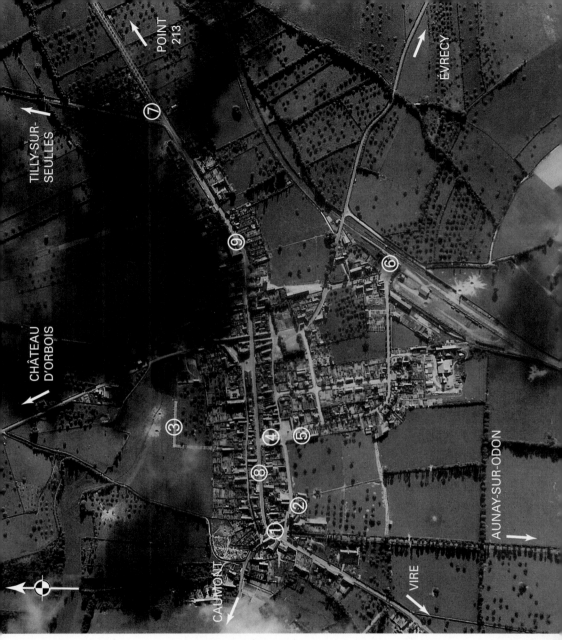

VILLERS-BOCAGE, 12 JUNE 1944

Villers-Bocage from the air. This aerial photograph was taken on the morning of 12 June. Note the anti-tank ditch just to the north of the little town, designed to prevent any outflanking movement as this was a 'rear entrance' into Panzer Lehr Division's positions.

(Keele University Photo Archive)

① Place Jeanne d'Arc
② Church
③ Anti-tank ditch (incomplete)
④ Town hall
⑤ Post office
⑥ Railway station
⑦ Calvary
⑧ Rue Pasteur
⑨ Rue Georges Clemenceau (RN 175)

TILLY-SUR-SEULLES

POINT 213

ÉVRECY

CHÂTEAU D'ORBOIS

AUNAY-SUR-ODON

CAUMONT

VIRE

Canadian sector in the east would soak up the 'hard pounding' of the anticipated German counter-attacks, in order to make it easier for the Americans in the west to achieve the major breakout (Operation 'Cobra'). Nevertheless, Operation 'Perch', as the initial XXX Corps assault was code-named, was not going well and it was time to do something spectacular in order to break the logjam. The result was the daring 'Right Hook' manoeuvre aimed at Villers-Bocage and the vital high ground to its north-east. This was to be achieved by Monty's tried and trusted 'Old Guard', the divisions which had served him so well in North Africa, foremost amongst them being the famous 'Desert Rats', 7th Armoured Division, which had come ashore on 7 June and was yet to be fully involved in operations.

This is the story of that right hook and of the other battles that took place south of Bayeux and Caen, around Tilly-sur-Seulles, during the all-important two weeks after the landings. I have tried to explain how such factors as the morale of the troops, the quality of their commanders and the unfortunate shortcomings of British tank design all played their part in the drama, as did the close-confining *bocage* countryside, which helped the defence more than anything else, apart perhaps from the battle expertise

A knocked-out Tiger in the streets of Villers-Bocage after the second phase of the battle for the town. This is the farthest west any German tank penetrated during this part of the battle. The tank was one of the three set on fire by Lieutenant Cotton and Sergeant Bramall, to prevent their recovery by the Germans. (*Bundesarchiv 101/494/3376/13a*)

Two panzergrenadiers unconcernedly light cigarettes after the British forces withdrew from Villers-Bocage. The wrecked Cromwell tanks of Captain Dyas and RSM Holloway are behind them. *(Bundesarchiv 101/738/275/17a)*

of the enemy panzergrenadiers and tank crews. I have also endeavoured to compare two tank engagements in which the ability and bravery of a single tank commander and his crew, in one case German, in the other British, played a major part in the outcome. This has been done within the framework of the 'Battle Zone Normandy' series, providing glimpses of the individual soldier's battles rather than just the 'bigger picture'.

ACKNOWLEDGEMENTS

I have many people to thank for their kind assistance with this book, in particular: Monsieur Henri Marie, local historian of Villers-Bocage and undoubted expert on the battle. In addition to kindly giving me help he has also generously agreed to assist visitors (please see page 122). I must also thank: Dr Jean Pierre Benamou OBE, MSM, MT, Conservateur du Musée Memorial de la Bataille de Normandie; Mademoiselle Agnès Therese, Office de Tourisme du Pre-Bocage; *Oberst aD* Helmut Ritgen, late Panzer

Lehr Division; Douglas Allen, late 4th County of London Yeomanry, and other Old Comrades of the Sharpshooters; Alec Armitage, son of the late Major-General G.T.A. Armitage; David Fletcher, Tank Museum historian; Merlin Milner, son of the late Major Christopher Milner MC; Cecil Newton of The Creully Club (4th/7th Royal Dragoon Guards 1940–45 Association); Major Boris Mollo TD, historian of the Sharpshooters; Mrs Valerie Nevitt, daughter of the late Squadron Quartermaster-Sergeant Wilf Harris DCM; Dr Simon Trew, the ever helpful and patient series editor; the staffs of the Public Record Office, the Imperial War Museum Photographic Library, the National Army Museum, the Green Jackets Museum and the Durham Light Infantry Museum; the MoD Whitehall Library; Home Headquarters 4th/7th Royal Dragoon Guards; Frau Martina Caspers of the Bundesarchiv; Winston Ramsey, editor-in-chief of 'After The Battle', and Daniel Taylor whose definitive book on Villers-Bocage was published by them; my wife Anne and son Jonathan who accompanied me on our 'tour of the *bocage*' – how different it is now to the summer of 1944; and finally, Viscount David Montgomery for writing the Foreword. Thank you all for your generous assistance.

George Forty
Bryantspuddle, Dorset, 2004

The cost of the battle. The Tilly-sur-Seulles War Cemetery holds 1,222 graves (British, New Zealand, Canadian, Australian and German). *(Author)*

PART TWO

HISTORY

CHAPTER 1

THE BEACHHEAD

On 6 June 1944, between the hours of 0630 and 0800, five infantry divisions – two American, two British and one Canadian – landed on five carefully selected beaches, over an 80-kilometre (km) stretch of the Normandy coast, between Ouistreham at the mouth of the River Orne in the east and Quinéville on the east coast of the Cotentin Peninsula in the west. Code-named 'Sword', 'Juno', 'Gold', 'Omaha' and 'Utah', the beaches have long since taken their place in the annals of military history, as have the daring airborne landings that preceded them. Airborne troops from one British and two American airborne divisions landed to secure the flanks of the beachhead area, destroy vital bridges, gun positions and so on. The amphibious landings took place at half-tide so as to strike a happy medium between low tide, when there would have been far too much bullet-swept open beach for the attackers to cross, and high tide, when all the highly lethal beach obstacles would have been hidden under the waves. Operation 'Neptune', the assault phase of 'Overlord', which was the result of months of careful planning and preparation, was a dazzling success, and despite all the odds against such an invasion, Hitler's supposedly impregnable Atlantic Wall was breached.

By the end of D-Day, some 155,000 troops were ashore and, with the protection afforded by almost continuous naval and air operations from the 5,000-plus warships and other naval craft in the invasion area, together with more than 5,000 fighter and ground attack aircraft and an equal number of bombers providing air cover round the clock, they were definitely there to stay. Omaha had been the most difficult landing beach to secure and 1st US Infantry Division, in particular, had suffered many casualties. It had not reached all its initial objectives, but it was, nevertheless, firmly established everywhere. In the British/ Canadian sector, the leading troops were, on average, some

Above: Coming ashore from the massive open doors of a tank landing ship is a Crusader III, AA Mark II, armed with twin 20-mm Oerlikon AA cannon. The tank, named *Allakeefek* (from an Arabic expression adapted into British soldiers' slang, roughly equivalent to the modern 'no worries'), belonged to 22nd Armoured Brigade headquarters. *(IWM B5129)*

Page 17: A Sherman tank of 4th/7th Dragoon Guards (Corporal Johnson's of Lieutenant Morrison's troop) knocked out close to Lingèvres church on 14 June. *(IWM B5783)*

10 km inland, although the important city of Caen was still in German hands. Casualties had been much lighter than expected, whilst the remarkable armoured fighting vehicles of British 79th Armoured Division – Hobart's 'Funnies' – had more than proved their worth.

Here Monty is inspecting men of 4th CLY in their camp near Thetford in Norfolk. Behind him is Lt-Col the Viscount Arthur Cranley (later Earl of Onslow), who had commanded 4th CLY since the end of the North African campaign. *(IWM H36004)*

Field Marshal Montgomery later wrote:

'We had achieved surprise, the troops had fought magnificently and our losses had been much lower than had ever seemed possible. We had breached the Atlantic Wall along the whole "Neptune" frontage and all assaulting divisions were ashore... To sum up, the results of D-Day were extremely encouraging, although the weather remained a great anxiety.'

Source: B.L. Montgomery, *Normandy to the Baltic*, pp. 48–9.

The story of the planning, build-up and assault on these beaches has already been the subject of earlier volumes in the 'Battle Zone Normandy' series. Now it is time to continue the story into the Normandy countryside. The overall plan that General Montgomery had outlined to all his senior commanders, together with a number of VIPs including HM King George VI, Prime Minister Churchill and the Supreme Commander, General Eisenhower, at a famous meeting on 15 May, had the following broad aims:

- To penetrate to an average depth of some 15 km on D-Day, capturing the towns of Isigny-sur-Mer, Bayeux and Caen.
- By D+9, to have taken the high ground running from St-Lô, through Caumont-l'Éventé and on to Villers-Bocage; additionally, if possible, to have secured the port of Cherbourg.
- By D+50 to have broken out from this area, first to the south and south-west, then swinging east. This would require the British and Canadian armies to draw in as many as possible of the German reserves – in particular the armoured units – to the eastern side of the beachhead, so as to make it easier for the Americans to break out in the west.

Coming ashore on Gold Beach. This 5th RTR M3A3 Stuart V was 'drowned' in the surf during the tricky period of getting from the landing craft to the beach on 7 June. This M3A3 has had its two original sponson-mounted machine guns removed. Note also the two formation signs on the front mudguards – 7th Armoured Division's Desert Rat on one, 22nd Armoured Brigade's Stag's Head on the other. *(IWM A23946)*

Lieutenant General Omar N. Bradley, commander of First US Army, described this most succinctly when he remembered what was said at Monty's briefing:

'During our battle for Normandy, the British and Canadian armies were to decoy the enemy reserves and to draw them to their front on the extreme eastern edge of the Allied beachhead. Thus while Monty taunted the enemy at Caen, we were to make our break on the long roundabout road to Paris. When reckoned in terms of national pride, this decoy mission became a sacrificial one, for while we tramped around the outside flank, the British were to sit in place and pin down the Germans. Yet strategically it fitted into a logical division of labours, for it was toward Caen that the enemy reserves would race once the alarm was sounded.'

Source: Omar N. Bradley, *A Soldier's Story*, p. 241.

This has been quoted in full from Bradley's own words because so much has subsequently been written as to whether or not Monty followed his 'master plan' or whether, in his subsequent memoirs and with hindsight, he made it seem to fit the situation that developed. It is not an argument which needs to be discussed further here except to say that, if Bradley, who was invariably one of Montgomery's severest critics, believed from the outset that the master plan was being followed, then that should be sufficient to silence the arguments once and for all.

Provided all went well, by D+90, the Allied armies would be established along the line of the River Seine and northern France would next be liberated.

This then was the overall plan and its immediate initial success depended upon taking Caen and the surrounding area, with armoured columns penetrating inland to gain space and, as Monty put it, 'to peg out claims well inland'. And of course, whilst doing this, they had to tie down as many of the German reserves as possible.

Thus, having achieved their first tenuous toehold, then successfully secured and linked up the various individual beachheads, it was now time for the Allied forces to begin pushing out in order to expand the beachhead sufficiently before the defenders could launch a sizeable counter-stroke. There were a number of reasons why the Germans had been prevented from mounting an immediate major counter-attack. First and foremost was the Allies' total air supremacy over the battlefield area. This would cause the commander of Army Group B, *Generalfeldmarschall* (Field Marshal) Erwin Rommel, to make a formal complaint to the *Luftwaffe* (the German Air Force) regarding the lack of support that his hard-pressed troops were receiving.

While the Germans were trying to assemble their counter-strokes against the landings, they were harassed, delayed and severely disorganised by continual air attacks. Another reason for the German failure to respond to Rommel's battle cry to fight the major battle on the beaches (or as he put it: '*Die HKL [Haupt Kampf Linie] ist der Strand!*' or 'The main line of resistance is the beach!') was entirely of their own making – namely the command and control arrangements for the all-important armour.

Generalfeldmarschall Erwin Rommel, Commander Army Group B, receives his field marshal's baton from Adolf Hitler. He was promoted to field marshal and awarded the Diamonds to his Knight's Cross after capturing Tobruk in June 1942. After North Africa, he was responsible for strengthening the Atlantic Wall and commanded the German defence in Normandy, until seriously wounded when his staff car was strafed by Allied fighters on 17 July 1944. *(IWM HU17207)*

There was no disagreement that the ten panzer divisions and one panzergrenadier division supporting the forces in the west, with a tank strength of over 1,500, which at the time represented 30 per cent of the entire strength of the German armoured forces, would play a major role – indeed possibly the most decisive – against any invasion. There were, however, major disagreements on how they should be commanded, controlled and deployed. Rommel wanted them close to the coastline, so that they could be brought into action immediately and would not have to be moved forward to the battle area under adverse air conditions – his own bitter experience in North Africa coming to the fore. However, *General der Panzertruppen* (General of Armoured Troops) Leo Freiherr Geyr von Schweppenburg, who commanded Panzer Group West and who was expected to control most of the armour in the event of an invasion, had been used to a far easier air situation on the Eastern Front and had entirely different ideas. He had been determined to keep the bulk of the armour concentrated and away from the beaches, able to be switched to the main invasion front once that had been determined. Commander-in-Chief West (OB West), Field Marshal Gerd von Rundstedt, and the Supreme Commander, Adolf Hitler, vacillated between the two, being unable to decide on which was the most likely area for the major Allied landings. Even when the Allies had landed, many of the senior German commanders still thought that Normandy might be only a feint and that the main thrust would still be in the Pas de Calais area. Consequently Rommel had only limited resources where it mattered when the moment for action arose.

The elderly *Generalfeldmarschall* Gerd von Rundstedt, C-in-C West, was one of the Third Reich's senior commanders. Orthodox, competent but uninspiring, he had originally retired in 1938 but was recalled to help plan the invasion of Poland. In and out of favour with Hitler, he was C-in-C West until July 1944, when he was sacked for clashing with Hitler's 'no withdrawals' policy. Reinstated two months later, he served until March 1945 when he was sacked again. *(IWM AP47832)*

Additionally, all the senior German commanders were bedevilled by Hitler's 'no withdrawal' policy, in which he had ordered that every German serviceman must fight where he stood to the last bullet and grenade, with no question of withdrawing to a new line of resistance. Although both von Rundstedt and Rommel realised the stupidity of following such restrictive orders, they felt they had to abide by them. Thus the

German defensive tactics were inevitably based on last-minute *ad hoc* plans, depending upon how the situation developed, rather than any well thought out fluid type of defence. Reserves were committed on an as-needed basis rather than according to any sensible, properly thought out plan. Also, it led to the most precious reserves – the panzer divisions – being brought into the line to replace or bolster up shattered infantry units. Although, as is evidenced by the success of Panzer Lehr Division south of Bayeux and Caen, they performed extremely well, they were unable for the most part to use their most important battle winning attributes of mobility, protection and firepower. They were, however, aided by the nature of the *bocage*, which favoured the defender and made life extremely difficult for the attacker,

General der Panzertruppen Leo Freiherr Geyr von Schweppenburg, C-in-C Panzer Group West, whose autocratic hold over the reserve panzers infuriated Rommel. His headquarters was almost wiped out by British fighter-bombers on 10 June. *(Helmut Ritgen)*

especially when Allied armour was up against well-trained panzergrenadiers with a range of man-portable, anti-tank weapons.

Despite these restrictions on the Germans, the Allies had not had an easy time of it either and, in the British sector, the all-important city of Caen was still firmly in German hands. Bayeux had, however, been liberated on D+1 by 50th Infantry Division, and Montgomery was confident that his 'grand design' could still be achieved.

The 21st century view of open, rolling countryside, looking on down the route by which 7th Armoured Division advanced towards Villers-Bocage. The view is along the D71 road after Briquessard looking towards Amayé-sur-Seulles. The vista now is much more open than it would have been in 1944. *(Author)*

TROOPS INVOLVED

Before getting down to looking in more detail at what would take place in the period prior to 7th Armoured Division's daring thrust to Villers-Bocage, it is helpful first to examine the troops who would be involved in the operation.

The main British units involved were 7th Armoured and 50th Infantry Divisions which, together with 49th Infantry Division, made up Lieutenant-General (Lt-Gen) G.C. Bucknall's XXX Corps, part of Lt-Gen Sir Miles Dempsey's Second (British) Army. 6th, 8th and 9th Durham Light Infantry (DLI) comprised 151st Infantry Brigade of 50th Infantry Division, which features in

Battlefield Tour C, and had landed on Gold Beach on D-Day. They had faced some resistance, but were firmly established ashore by midday and by last light had a secure bridgehead some distance inland. 4th/7th Royal Dragoon Guards, one of the armoured regiments of 8th Armoured Brigade, which would be supporting the Durham Brigade at Lingèvres and les Verrières (*see Tour C, pages 161–82*), had also come ashore on D-Day, in support and initially under command of 69th Infantry Brigade. 7th Armoured Division, however, did not come ashore until 7 June, also landing at Gold Beach, and then moving to a concentration area at Caugy and from there to occupy positions in the Mendaye area. Among other later arrivals was 49th Infantry Division. All would be involved in the heavy fighting south and south-east of Bayeux as the British and Canadians sought to enlarge their beachhead.

BRITISH PERSONALITIES

Sir Miles Dempsey had fought in the First World War as a junior officer in the Royal Berkshire Regiment and came to prominence in the Second World war as a staunch supporter of Montgomery. He had commanded 13th Infantry Brigade in the British Expeditionary Force in 1940 and XIII Corps of the Eighth Army during the closing stages of the North African campaign and in Sicily and Italy, returning with Monty for the Normandy invasion. Tall, athletic, able yet modest, he has never been widely known to the public, but proved himself to be a competent, 'safe pair of hands', while commanding Second (British) Army in North-West Europe.

Not so Bucknall, who had also been brought back from Italy to command XXX Corps. 'Bucknall is very weak and I am quite certain unfit to command a corps' – so wrote a worried Field Marshal Sir Alan Brooke, Chief of the Imperial General Staff, in his diary on 7 April 1944, having attended one of Monty's briefings. Bucknall would soon prove to be too indecisive and lacking in imagination when faced with a crisis. As we shall see, he would lose his command because of the Villers-Bocage débâcle, as would both the much-respected Major-General (Maj-Gen) Bobbie Erskine (commander of 7th Armoured Division) and the equally able Brigadier 'Looney' Hinde (of 22nd Armoured Brigade) who would inevitably also get the blame for what happened.

Lt-Gen Sir Miles Dempsey, Commander Second (British) Army, (in the centre) is seen here with two of his corps commanders, Lt-Gen Sir John Crocker (I Corps) and Lt-Gen Gerry Bucknall (XXX Corps) – in beret. They were photographed at Ranville on 10 June. *(IWM B5326)*

Opposing forces

On the 'other side of the hill', the German forces can be broken down into two elements. First were the coastal garrison troops manning both the beach defences of the Atlantic Wall and providing in depth the immediate counter-attack forces. It was *General der Artillerie* (General of Artillery) Erich Marcks' LXXXIV Corps that bore the brunt of the D-Day landings, in particular 352nd Infantry Division (*Generalleutnant* [GenLt] Dietrich Kraiss) and part of 709th Infantry Division (GenLt Karl-Wilhelm von Schlieben) on the left opposite First US Army and 716th Infantry Division (GenLt Wilhelm Richter) opposite Second (British) Army.

The other infantry divisions in Marcks' corps were all too far away to affect matters, 243rd being in the Western Cotentin, whilst 319th (the largest division in the German Army) was garrisoning the Channel Islands. Marcks was a tough, energetic commander (despite having a wooden leg) and a firm friend of Rommel, whose Army Group B commanded Seventh Army (defending the Channel Coast from Brittany to the River Seine), Fifteenth Army (Channel and North Sea coasts between the Seine and the Scheldt), and LXXXVIII Corps in the Netherlands.

All Rommel had as an immediate counter-attack force in the Caen area was a single panzer division, 21st Panzer Division (GenLt Edgar Feuchtinger), positioned between Caen and Falaise. The new 21st Panzer Division (the original 21st Panzer Division had been destroyed in Tunisia in May 1943) came into existence in Normandy in mid-1943. Although the division contained some *Afrika Korps* veterans, its equipment included a number of obsolescent French tanks and it had been rated as unfit for service on the Eastern Front.

Stronger forces were, however, not too far away: for example, 12th SS Panzer Division *Hitlerjugend* (*SS-Gruppenführer* [Major-General] Fritz Witt – killed by Allied naval gunfire on 14 June) being at Verneuil-sur-Avre and Panzer Lehr Division near Nogent le Rotrou, some 120 km south-west of Paris. The former was, as its name implies, recruited from Hitler Youth members in 1943, when the average age of its new soldiers was only 17. Initially a training unit, it was sent to Belgium in 1943 and to France in April 1944. It fought with fanatical bravery and some skill, having been rushed to Normandy, but suffered heavy casualties. After Witt was killed his place would be taken by one of Germany's most colourful young panzer soldiers, Kurt 'Panzer' Meyer, who became the youngest divisional commander in the Third Reich. Formed from the demonstration (*Lehr*) units of the panzer training schools at Potsdam and the Bergen Manoeuvre Area, GenLt Fritz Bayerlein's Panzer Lehr Division was one of the strongest divisions in the German Army, with a total of 237 tanks and assault guns and 658 half-tracked vehicles – double the normal panzer division's number of half-tracks. However, it and 12th SS Panzer were part of the German reserve and not available for action without explicit permission from Hitler himself.

After the planned immediate counter-attack had been aborted, Panzer Lehr Division took up positions opposite XXX Corps. At the same time, opposite I Corps were 12th SS Panzer and 21st Panzer Divisions, bolstering up what remained of 716th Infantry Division around Caen. In other words, instead of the panzers being available for an armoured counter-attack to recapture Bayeux and drive the Allied landing forces into the sea, they were reduced to a more static defence, while the chain of command

Order of Battle: Panzer Lehr Division
10 June 1944

Commander — *Generalleutnant Fritz Bayerlein*

Division Headquarters
    130th (mot) Mapping Detachment
    Divisional Escort Company
    130th (mot) Military Police Troop

130th Panzer Regiment — *Oberst Rudolf Gerhardt*
    Regimental Staff Company
    1st Panzer Battalion, 6th Panzer Regt — *Major Markowski*
      (seconded from 3rd Panzer Division)
    2nd Panzer Battalion (Panzer IV) — *Oberstleutnant Prinz Wilhelm von Schönburg-Waldenburg*

    316th Radio-Controlled Company

901st Panzergrenadier Demonstration Regiment — *Oberst Georg Scholze*

    Regimental Staff Company
    1st Panzergrenadier Battalion — *Major Konrad Uthe*
    2nd Panzergrenadier Battalion — *Major Schöne*
    Self-propelled Infantry Gun Company
    Engineer Company
    Flak Company (Light)

became more and more complicated. Von Schweppenburg commented bitterly that, at a time when everything depended upon swift action, orders were being issued to the small number of panzer divisions then available by no fewer than six different headquarters: *SS-Obergruppenführer* Dietrich's I SS Panzer Corps, his own Panzer Group West, *Generaloberst* (Colonel-General) Friedrich Dollmann's Seventh Army, Rommel's Army Group B, von Rundstedt's OB West and Hitler's Armed Forces High Command in Berlin!

SS-Obergruppenführer (Lt-Gen) Josef 'Sepp' Dietrich was the rough, tough commander of I SS Panzer Corps. One time chauffeur and bodyguard to Hitler, his bravery was unquestionable. Although he would go on to command Sixth Panzer Army and be awarded the coveted Diamonds to his Knight's Cross in August 1944, one of only 27 to gain this honour, his ability as a field commander was always suspect and he relied very heavily on carefully chosen subordinates to keep him on the right track, whilst he remained an admirable

902nd Panzergrenadier Demonstration Regiment

Oberstleutnant Willi Welsch

Regimental Staff Company
1st Panzergrenadier Battalion   *Major Zwierzynski*
2nd Panzergrenadier Battalion   *Hauptmann Müller*
Self-propelled Infantry Gun Company, Engineer Company

130th Panzer Artillery Regiment   *Major Zeisler*

1st Panzer Artillery Battalion (temporarily unavailable)
2nd Panzer Artillery Battalion
3rd Panzer Artillery Battalion
992nd Medium Artillery Battalion (attached)

130th Panzer Reconnaissance Demonstration Battalion

Major Gerd von Fallois

130th Anti-Tank Demonstration Battalion *Major Joachim Barth*

311th Army Anti-Aircraft Battalion

130th Panzer Engineer Battalion   *Major Herbert Eltrich*

130th Panzer Signals Battalion

130th Field Replacement Battalion

Support Units

130th Supply Troop, 130th Truck Park, 130th (mot) Bakery Company,
130th (mot) Butcher Company, 130th (mot) Divisional Administration
Company, 130th Medical Battalion, 130th (mot) Field Post Office

figurehead, admired and respected by his troops. He was thus very different to the aristocratic Geyr von Schweppenburg. Brave and highly experienced, von Schweppenburg was also extremely stubborn and refused to accept Rommel's authority. He would survive the war and become an accomplished military commentator and historian. Fritz Bayerlein was, of course, one of Rommel's protégés, and had been his chief of staff in North Africa, before commanding 3rd Panzer Division in Russia. He commanded Panzer Lehr Division brilliantly, Rommel once describing him as being, 'a stocky, tough little terrier of a man, full of energy and enthusiasm'.

Although their complicated chain of command made life difficult for the German troops on the ground, their superior tanks and battle experience made them formidable adversaries – and none were more lethal than the Panthers of Panzer Lehr Division and the Tigers of the *Waffen-SS*. So before describing the lead-up to the Villers-Bocage and Lingèvres battles, it is useful to look further at the organisation and equipment of both sides.

Sherman VC Firefly, its massive 17-pounder gun barrel overhanging the front of the tank. Initially, there were only enough Fireflies to issue them on a scale of one per troop in British armoured regiments. They provided the only big 'punch' in the tank troops of 7th Armoured Division. *(IWM B51300)*

The first thing to consider is the state of mind of the troops who would be mainly involved in these operations. From the outset the ex-Eighth Army troops, in particular 7th Armoured Division, had their problems.

7th Armoured Division's commanding officer, Maj-Gen 'Bobbie' Erskine, later wrote:

'When the division arrived [in the UK from Italy] in early January they had to have their leave. We then had to draw complete new equipment for the entire division as we had left all our own in Italy. This in itself is a fairly major undertaking. It did not make matters easier when we found that the armoured brigade was to be equipped with

General Montgomery and Maj-Gen Bobbie Erskine, commander of 7th Armoured Division, photographed during the hectic period prior to D-Day, when Monty went around giving 'pep talks' to all the units which would land in Normandy on D-Day or just after. *(IWM H36006)*

Cromwells which was an entirely new tank for us. We knew the Sherman inside out, but none of us knew the Cromwell. This had various repercussions. The armoured regiments had to learn the gunnery and maintenance of a new tank which many judged inferior to the Sherman. Many of the Cromwells suffered from minor defects and the reputation of the tank did not improve as we had to repair the defects ourselves. The armoured regiments all had to go to Scotland (Kirkcudbright) to do their gunnery, which was absolutely necessary, but took up much time on a form of training which could have been avoided if we had been given Shermans...

Morale was as always a very important factor. The division contained many people who had been in it since 1941, who had seen the North African campaign through and had done Salerno. There was undoubtedly a feeling amongst a few that it was time somebody else had a go... There was a fundamental difference between troops like 7th Armoured Division who had been fighting continuously and fresh troops who had never been in action. The latter wanted to "win their spurs" and were ready to take on anything without question – once or twice. With 7th Armoured Division it was no use trying to pull wool over their eyes. They knew war too well to take it light-heartedly or carelessly. We left for Normandy with a high state of morale, but it is no use concealing the fact that we felt we had been rushed. We were nothing like so well teamed up as we had been before Salerno.'

Source: Letter held by Tank Museum Library.

Order of Battle: 7th Armoured Division

General Officer Commanding	*Maj-Gen G.W.E.J. Erskine*
GSO 1	*Lt-Col N.M.H. Wall*
22nd Armoured Brigade	*Brigadier W.R.N. Hinde*
1st Royal Tank Regiment	*Lt-Col R.M.P. Carver*
5th Royal Tank Regiment	*Lt-Col C.H. Holliman*
4th County of London Yeomanry (The Sharpshooters)	
	Lt-Col Viscount A. Cranley
1st Btn, The Rifle Brigade (Motor)	*Lt-Col A.G.V. Paley*
131st (Queen's) Infantry Brigade	*Brigadier M.S. Ekins*
1st/5th Battalion, The Queen's Royal Regiment (West Surrey)	
	Lt-Col H. Wood
1st/6th Battalion, The Queen's Royal Regiment (West Surrey)	
	Lt-Col M. Forrester
1st/7th Battalion, The Queen's Royal Regiment (West Surrey)	
	Lt-Col D.S. Gordon

Independent Machine-Gun Company
3rd Support Company, The Royal Northumberland Fusiliers

Armoured Reconnaissance Regiment
8th King's Royal Irish Hussars   *Lt-Col C. Goulburn*

Royal Armoured Corps
263rd Forward Delivery Squadron

Matters were also not made any easier when various key senior officers were taken away to spread their battle experience to other divisions. For example, the commander of 131st Infantry Brigade (Brigadier L.G. 'Bolo' Whistler), the division's GSO 1 (the senior staff officer), and the chief signals officer, together with a number of others, were all posted elsewhere.

Thus, while 7th Armoured and 50th Infantry Divisions, which together made up Montgomery's 'ex-Desert Rats' contingent, were his most experienced troops, they had difficulties from the outset. However, this should not get out of proportion. All the 'Desert Rats' I have spoken to over the years have had no doubts in their minds that their divisions were 'ready, willing and able' to take on and beat the best that Hitler could bring against them.

It was perhaps unfortunate that 7th Armoured Division had to do so with a tank that was designed for the chase rather than the bitter, close range tank-versus-tank slog which was a feature of the *bocage* battles. They did have their 'Sunday punch' in the shape of the Sherman Firefly, but this was only at best a way of

Royal Artillery **Brigadier R. Mews**
- 3rd Royal Horse Artillery Lt-Col J.A. Norman
- 5th Royal Horse Artillery Lt-Col G.P. Gregson
- 15th Light Anti-Aircraft Regiment
- 65th Anti-Tank Regiment (The Norfolk Yeomanry)
  Lt-Col W.B. Stewart

Royal Engineers Lt-Col A.D. Hunter
- 4th, 621st Field Squadrons, 143rd Field Park Squadron

Royal Signals Lt-Col G.S. Knox
- 7th Armoured Division Signals

Royal Army Service Corps Lt-Col E.G. Hazelton
- 58th, 67th, 507th Companies

Royal Army Medical Corps Col E.C. Eccles
- 2nd Light Field Ambulance, 131st Field Ambulance,
- 29th Field Dressing Station, 70th Field Hygiene Section,
- 134th Mobile Dental Unit

Royal Army Ordnance Corps Lt-Col A.C. Lusty
- Divisional Ordnance Field Park

Royal Electrical and Mechanical Engineers
  Lt-Col J.D. Berryman
- 7th Armoured Troops Workshop, 22nd Armoured Brigade Workshop,
- 131st Brigade Workshop, 15th Light Anti-Aircraft Workshop

mounting a more powerful gun onto the Sherman, and only available in sufficient quantity to allow for one Firefly per tank troop. However, the British armoured regiments and lorried infantry battalions were fully mechanised, with plenty of artillery support, and did not have to rely upon horsed transport like much of the German Army. (Though this did not apply to their immediate opponents from Panzer Lehr, who were the *crème de la crème* of the German armoured forces.)

In support of Panzer Lehr at Villers-Bocage were sub-units of the formidable 101st Heavy SS Panzer Battalion with, when at full strength, three companies each of 14 Tiger I heavy tanks, plus another three in battalion headquarters. By the time this battalion got to the Normandy area it had suffered both from air attack and mechanical breakdowns, so none of the tank companies was at full strength. However, the Tiger had already achieved an awesome reputation, its firepower and protection making it possible for a small number of them to achieve the impossible – as Tour A graphically describes.

CHAPTER 2

HARD POUNDING

Most of 7th Armoured Division had landed successfully in France by the end of 7 June. Fortunately only a few vehicles were lost in the surf, and by that evening 22nd Armoured Brigade units were safely in their concentration area, apart from 1st Rifle Brigade which had yet to arrive from the beachhead, so that the following morning they were ready to support what were initially infantry operations in the main. The XXX Corps plan, Operation 'Perch', was that, having landed on Gold Beach, 50th Infantry Division would capture Bayeux, secure the road from there to Tilly-sur-Seulles, then break through the Panzer Lehr Division's defensive positions in the area of Tilly-sur-Seulles, Juvigny, Hottot-les-Bagues and la Senaudière. The initial attack would be supported by fire from a battleship and two cruisers as well as close air support. Once the way was clear, 7th Armoured Division would then pass through, take Villers-Bocage, and press on to Évrecy and the important high ground in its vicinity. This last manoeuvre was to be supported by an airborne landing by 1st Airborne Division (code-named 'Wild Oats'). Having secured a firm base in the district known as la Suisse Normande, the armour would then turn eastwards towards Thury-Harcourt and the Orne River crossings.

However, Air Chief Marshal Sir Trafford Leigh-Mallory, the allied air commander, categorically refused to transport 1st Airborne Division, saying that the operation as planned was just too dangerous for his pilots. This refusal infuriated Monty who described Leigh-Mallory as a 'gutless bugger' and argued (to no avail), that Leigh-Mallory sitting in his office could not know the local battle form. Fortunately for the future smooth co-operation of the Army and RAF, Monty's anger appears to have been just a flash in the pan and soon afterwards he was praising the airman as being a 'very genuine chap and will do anything he can to help with the war'.

Unfortunately, however, the local battlefield situation also soon worsened, because, after the fall of Bayeux without much opposition, 50th Infantry Division got itself bogged down in its attack in the Tilly-sur-Seulles area. This was principally due to the nature of the close *bocage* countryside which favoured the defence and the fact that the enemy troops were mainly from the formidable Panzer Lehr Division, adept in the use of their excellent Panther tanks and of such deadly short-range weapons as the *Panzerfaust* (a hand-held anti-tank weapon roughly equivalent to the British PIAT and the American bazooka). Lack of progress led Monty to decide to modify his strategy and to send 7th Armoured Division in a wide 'right hook' to capture Villers-Bocage and the high ground to its north-east, then to push on to Évrecy. Although it was clearly Monty's final decision to send the 'Desert Rats' right flanking, it is not entirely clear whose idea it actually was to undertake the 'right hook'. Everyone from Monty down to Maj-Gen Erskine claimed the idea as theirs.

As Major-General Erskine wrote in the post-war letter already quoted:

'After some unsuccessful stabs at Tilly, I suggested the use of the Division's mobility round the right flank of 50 Div. I was sure there was a soft spot here and had in fact reconnoitred routes and had a cut and dried plan for a swoop on Villers-Bocage. The plan was eventually accepted, but after much delay. It could have been carried out 24 hours earlier and those 24 hours were vital.'

En route for Normandy were train-loads of tanks, such as these Panthers. They had to travel by night because of Allied air superiority. Even then they were liable to sabotage from French resistance fighters. *(J-P. Benamou, via author's collection)*

A tank destroyer team, complete with *Panzerfausts*, ready to go out in a VW *Schwimmwagen* (the amphibious version of the *Kubelwagen*). The hollow-charge *Panzerfaust* rocket could penetrate up to 200 mm of armour. *(Helmut Ritgen)*

Meanwhile 'on the other side of the hill' things were not going all that smoothly either. On 7 June, Panzer Group West was ordered by OB West to mount a major counter-attack. At that time, however, two major components of the armoured force needed for such a decisive attack – Panzer Lehr and 12th SS Panzer Division – had not yet arrived on the battlefield, while the third armoured division, 21st Panzer Division, was already involved in fighting the defensive battle near the coast. This meant that the counter-attack had to be postponed.

Fresh orders were then issued on the evening of 7 June for the attack to take place on the following day. These ordered I SS

Panzer Corps, with the three divisions already mentioned under command, to advance from the Caen–Ste-Croix area into the Allied bridgehead towards Courseulles-sur-Mer, with the mission of capturing the line St-Aubin-sur-Mer–Creully. The left flank of the advance was to be the line Carcagny–Ellon–Trungy. The orders for the attack were disseminated to the divisions whilst they were still *en route*, but it was anticipated that they would be in their forward concentration area astride the Caen–Bayeux road, between Ste-Croix-Grande-Tonne in the west and Bretteville-l'Orgueilleuse in the east, by 0300 hours on 8 June.

During its journey forward from the Chartres area, Panzer Lehr Division had been ordered to move in daylight, despite Bayerlein's strong objections to the commander of Seventh Army. As a result, it lost around 100 vehicles of all types. As Bayerlein put it, 'These were serious losses for a division not yet in action.'

A German staff officer described these first air attacks:

'Our motorized columns were coiling along the road towards the invasion beaches. Then something happened that left us in a daze. Spurts of fire flicked along the column and splashes of dust on the road. Everyone was piling out of the vehicles and scuttling for the neighbouring fields. Several vehicles were already in flames. This attack ceased as suddenly as it had crashed upon us 15 minutes before. The men started drifting back to the column again, pale and shaky and wondering how they had survived this fiery rain of bullets. This had been our first experience with the *Jabos* [fighter-bombers]. The march column was now completely disrupted and every man was on his own, to pull out of this blazing column as best he could. And it was none too soon, because an hour later the whole thing started all over again, only much worse this time. When this attack was over, the length of the road was strewn with splintered anti-tank guns (the pride of our division), flaming motors and charred implements of war.'

The same officer went on to explain that the march had to be called off and all the vehicles hidden in the dense bushes or in farms. No one dared show himself in daylight and thereafter they only travelled by night, sticking to the back roads, which had high hedges and bushes.

HISTORY

To make matters worse these losses would all be in vain, because the planned attack never materialised. This was principally because of the almost continual attentions of the *Jabos* during daylight hours. It was also clearly due to 'the divergent influence of higher staff', as von Schweppenburg put it, graphically illustrated by the Panzer Lehr move.

The German divisions that were to have been involved in the armoured counter-stroke then went over to the defensive and while their superior armoured fighting vehicles and general battlefield expertise were instrumental in imposing delay on the Allies, there could now be no question of driving the invaders into the sea. Nevertheless, despite the saturation bombing and almost continuous naval gunfire support, the Allies made slow progress, thanks, as Rommel put it, to his troops fighting with 'the greatest doggedness and utmost pugnacity'.

Cromwell and Sherman tanks from 7th Armoured Division, still with their wading kit in place, move off from the beach to their concentration area further inland. *(IWM B5257)*

By 8 June, the British and Canadians had made some gradual progress towards Caen, but its capture still eluded them. Instead, the focus shifted to the XXX Corps front, where limited gains were being made toward Tilly-sur-Seulles. Nevertheless, it is no

Stuart V light tank of 7th Armoured Division (note the 'Desert Rat' sign at the top left of the front glacis). The photograph was taken somewhere in the *bocage* on 15 June 1944. *(IWM B5608)*

exaggeration to say that, without the participation of I SS Panzer Corps in the defence of Normandy, Montgomery's armies would have reached the Seine long before D+90. The *Hitlerjugend*'s actions in the first days of the invasion prevented the early fall of Caen, whilst Michael Wittmann's amazing performance at Villers-Bocage would help thwart the early British attempts to outflank the German defence in that area. Later, both divisions of the panzer corps halted Montgomery's subsequent attempts to outflank Caen, namely Operations 'Epsom' and 'Windsor'.

PANZER GROUP WEST BOMBED

One of the most important events influencing the enlargement of the Allied bridgehead occurred on the evening of 10 June, when the château at la Caine, some 6 km north-west of Thury-Harcourt, was engaged by a carefully-directed bomb and rocket attack. The target was the headquarters of General Geyr von

Schweppenburg's Panzer Group West and the results were significant – the chief of staff (*Generalmajor* Ritter von Dawans) and 17 other staff officers were killed, and many others, including von Schweppenburg, were wounded. All communications, and thus vital control over the all-important panzer divisions, were lost. Rommel must have smiled wryly when he heard the news, having tried for many months to persuade the difficult, self-opinionated Geyr von Schweppenburg about the potential dangers of operating under Allied air superiority. The attack was not merely a lucky strike on the part of the Allies, but rather a carefully planned and well executed operation using both bombs and rockets, which was directed with pinpoint accuracy, thanks to information obtained via the Ultra code-breaking service.

Royal Engineers clearing mines in Tilly-sur-Seulles, 19 June. *(IWM B5772)*

THE ADVANCE BEGINS

Thus it was that at 0545 hours on 10 June, with 4th County of London Yeomanry (CLY) leading, 22nd Armoured Brigade advanced on Tilly-sur-Seulles down the divisional centre line, which was the main road through Bayeux. The forward positions of 50th Infantry Division were some 5 km north of Tilly and first contact with the Germans was made at Bucéels about 2.5 km further on. 5th Royal Tank Regiment (RTR) had followed 4th CLY on the divisional centre line, then diverged to the west when it was south of Blary. This was in order to get the brigade onto a two-regiment front, 5th RTR being directed on the route Ellon–Folliot–les Verrières, some 2,000 metres to the west of 4th CLY.

This proved to be too close, as it did not give the armoured units sufficient room for manoeuvre. The aim was, however, to keep the two lines of advance as close together as possible due to the extreme thickness of the *bocage* countryside. 5th RTR soon made contact with panzergrenadiers guarding road blocks in the Ellon area and could only make slow progress. This was because of the sunken lanes and the fact that the regiment's task was to eliminate all the Germans on its front and avoid leaving any pockets behind – not easy in the thick *bocage*. There was definitely a need for more infantry, the initial 'balance' of the force being wrong (tank-heavy rather than infantry-heavy).

While this was taking place, 1st RTR, the last of 7th Armoured Division's armoured regiments to disembark, was meant to deploy to the area of Condé-sur-Seulles and prepare to guard the bridges over the River Aure as the advance continued. However, as this meant making an awkward move across the front, it was not carried out, principally because progress was slow enough to enable these bridges to be taken over by the follow-up brigade (56th Infantry Brigade). The divisional commander had also put an 8th Hussars squadron under the command of 22nd Armoured Brigade, but as there was no room to employ it in right flank protection, it initially remained north-east of Bayeux.

During this period there was a 'friendly fire' incident between 4th CLY and 8th Armoured Brigade, which resulted in the loss of two 4th CLY tanks. 'The lesson,' comments the brigade report, 'is that we should have sent a liaison officer to 8 Armd Brigade, who would have been on our frequency and responsible for keeping them fully informed of our forward locations.' Unfortunately, 22nd Armoured Brigade was short of both liaison officers and scout cars and had already sent a liaison officer to divisional headquarters. 'The first requirement is good tank recognition, and the second, good liaison,' the report concluded.

The leading British tanks had cleared Bucéels of German troops by last light. However, as was typical of *bocage* fighting, elements of Panzer Lehr Division later re-entered the village, so it

This Sherman, possibly an artillery OP tank, was photographed on 13 June, *en route* to Tilly-sur-Seulles. It is passing a knocked out Panzer IV Ausf H. More of this model were produced than any other Panzer IV (some 3,700). *(IWM B5446)*

had to be dealt with all over again. 4th CLY then leaguered for the night in the area of St-Bazire. Meanwhile 2nd Battalion, The Gloucestershire Regiment, (2nd Glosters) of 56th Infantry Brigade but presently under command of 7th Armoured Division, moved up to Jérusalem so as to be immediately available should an infantry attack be necessary, with one company dug-in north of Bucéels. 5th RTR spent the night in the Butte du Gros Orme area and 2nd Battalion, The Essex Regiment, also of 56th Infantry Brigade, remained in the area after clearing it of Germans.

On 11 June, Brigadier Hinde visited 4th CLY and 2nd Glosters, giving orders to both commanding officers to secure a bridgehead across the Ruisseau du Pont-Esprit stream with a view to further operations against Tilly-sur-Seulles. The nature of the countryside made the attack a predominantly infantry affair, but with tank and artillery support. It attained its first objective, the two bridges near Bucéels, 5th RTR then continuing the advance towards Tilly. However, on reaching the woods at les Verrières just to the north of the village, 5th RTR was held up by tanks and infantry, which 'roughly handled' a 1st Rifle Brigade motor platoon that was in the wood, and was then counter-attacked by infantry. Meanwhile, an 8th Hussars squadron, which had been brought up on the right flank of 5th RTR to the north-east of la Senaudière, was also held up by Germans in some strength with anti-tank guns.

Brigadier Hinde next decided to attack the woods with 2nd Essex, supported by 5th RTR and artillery, so as to secure the area as a 'jumping-off point' for an attack on Lingèvres. H-hour was to be 1300 hours. Unfortunately, for various reasons, the attack was delayed until 1830 hours and although it was then initially successful, 2nd Essex was counter-attacked by about 10 tanks, infantry and two flame-throwers and was forced to withdraw to the northern edge of the wood, which it held until morning. This counter-attack almost completely surrounded the British force.

Lieutenant-Colonel Charles W. Pearce, a 4th CLY lieutenant in 1944, witnessed the German counter-attack, and later recalled:

'There was a regiment of self-propelled anti-tank guns and over 100 Shermans. It was quite fantastic. The Tigers just drove round shooting up everything. They knocked out ten Shermans, four SP guns and an M10. One Tiger was knocked out. It seems extraordinary that, although our tank crews are first class, our tank guns are unable to penetrate the German armour. The position was restored by 2130 hrs and all was quiet. Next morning I came back to the Regiment who were near Bucéels... Everybody was getting very tired, very little chance of eating and practically no sleep.'

Source: Quoted in *The Sharpshooter* newsletter.

While one cannot question the fact that Pearce witnessed the German counter-attack, the strength he gives for the British force is certainly an exaggeration and his tank recognition is suspect. At that time there were only a handful of Tigers in Normandy (316th Panzer Company attached to Panzer Lehr Regiment had three Tiger Is), and it is doubtful whether they would have been

HISTORY

used in such a task. They would later be joined by three heavy tank battalions of the *Waffen-SS* (101st and 102nd Heavy SS Panzer Battalions had Tiger Is and 503rd Battalion had a company of the even more powerful Tiger II *Königstiger*). It is more likely that the tanks were Panthers or even H or J models of the Panzer IV, both of which were more powerful than most Allied tanks, as is explained in the boxes on pages 71 and 85 which describe the main types of tank used by both sides.

Pearce goes on to compare the conditions with those when his unit had been surrounded in a desert battle as it seemed that, on this occasion too, there was no hope of relief. However, he comments wryly that at least in the desert it was possible to 'brew up' and eat, while in the *bocage* there were always snipers and the close country meant that enemy infantry could creep up unseen. This made it impossible for crews to get out of their tanks safely.

A *bocage* hedgerow provides some protection for this scared group of women and children, forced out of their homes by the fighting. *(IWM B5607)*

At midday on the 11th, XXX Corps decided that 56th Infantry Brigade's commander, Brigadier E.C. Pepper, should conduct operations on the main divisional centre line, while 22nd Armoured Brigade's Brigadier Hinde commanded the right-hand advance through Lingèvres. Therefore, 4th CLY came under command of 56th Infantry Brigade and 2nd Essex under 22nd Armoured Brigade. At this time 7th Armoured Division's integral infantry (131st Infantry Brigade) was still concentrating in the Bayeux area, so it was not yet available for action.

British infantrymen slog past a knocked-out Panther tank, near Bernières on 14 June. *(IWM B5534)*

THE 'RIGHT HOOK'

Corps HQ next ordered that 131st Infantry Brigade, with 1st RTR under command, should pass through 56th Infantry Brigade on the centre line Tilly-sur-Seulles–Villers-Bocage at first light on 12 June, while 22nd Armoured Brigade would protect the right flank. However, owing to the difficult country and the consequently slow progress, the fateful decision was made to pass 7th Armoured Division around the left flank of Panzer Lehr Division. 7th Armoured Division would approach Villers-Bocage from the west, that is, in the gap between the British and American sectors, close to the army boundary. By now the Americans were just north of Caumont-l'Évente and there appeared to be good prospects of exploiting that success in the direction of Villers-Bocage and even, if possible, of occupying the important high ground around what was known as Point 213 in 1944 (Point 217 on modern maps) some 2.5 km to the north-east of Villers-Bocage.

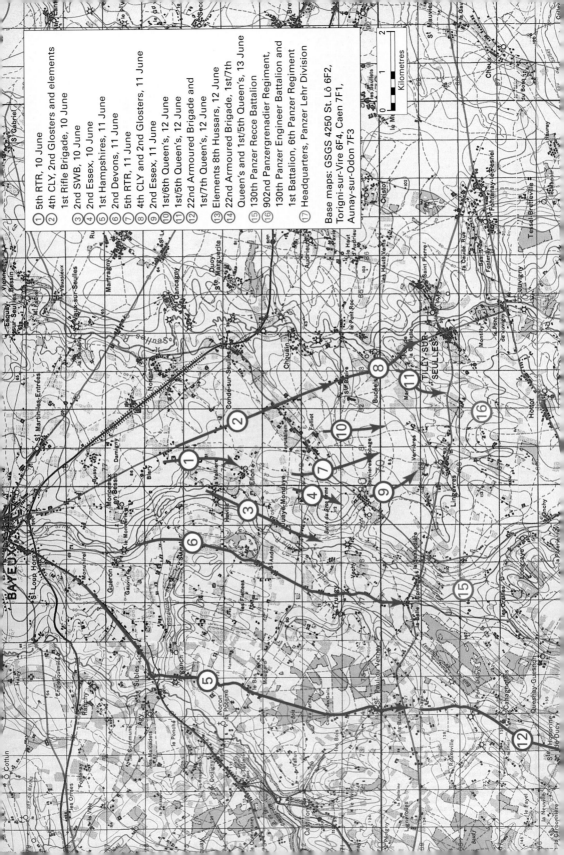

① 5th RTR, 10 June
② 4th CLY, 2nd Glosters and elements 1st Rifle Brigade, 10 June
③ 2nd SWB, 10 June
④ 2nd Essex, 10 June
⑤ 1st Hampshires, 11 June
⑥ 2nd Devons, 11 June
⑦ 5th RTR, 11 June
⑧ 4th CLY and 2nd Glosters, 11 June
⑨ 2nd Essex, 11 June
⑩ 1st/6th Queen's, 12 June
⑪ 1st/5th Queen's, 12 June
⑫ 22nd Armoured Brigade and 1st/7th Queen's, 12 June
⑬ Elements 8th Hussars, 12 June
⑭ 22nd Armoured Brigade, 1st/7th Queen's and 1st/5th Queen's, 13 June
⑮ 130th Panzer Recce Battalion
⑯ 902nd Panzergrenadier Regiment, 130th Panzer Engineer Battalion and 1st Battalion, 6th Panzer Regiment
⑰ Headquarters, Panzer Lehr Division

Base maps: GSGS 4250 St. Lô 6F2, Torigni-sur-Vire 6F4, Caen 7F1, Aunay-sur-Odon 7F3

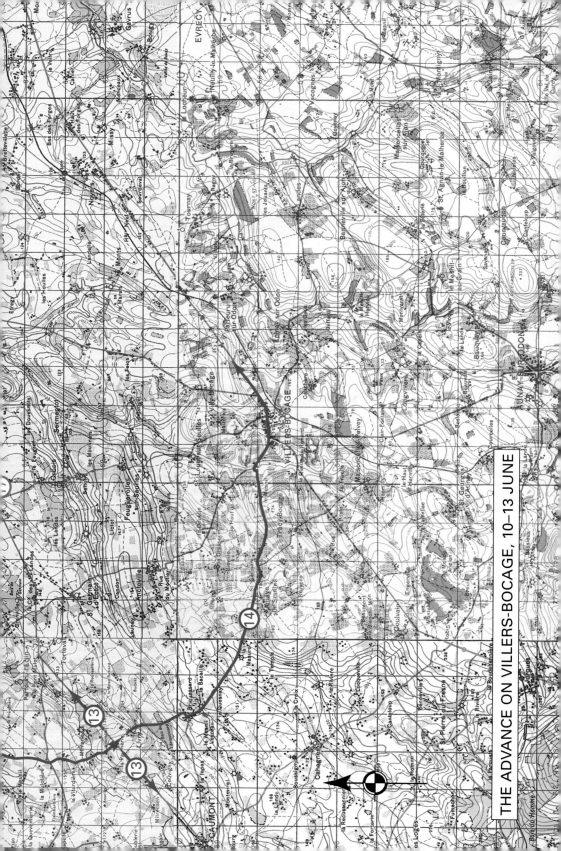

THE ADVANCE ON VILLERS-BOCAGE, 10–13 JUNE

'Mines in Verges'. A warning notice being erected on the outskirts of Tilly-sur-Seulles. *(IWM B5778)*

22nd Armoured Brigade, less 1st RTR, now had the following additional troops under command: 260th Anti-Tank Battery (with self–propelled 17-pounders), 8th Hussars (less one squadron), one squadron of 11th Hussars (but not until the evening of 12 June) and 1st/7th Battalion, The Queen's Royal Regiment (West Surrey). The 8th Hussars moved off about 1400 hours on 12 June and pushed out west to the crossroads just north of Trungy and then across to St-Paul-du-Vernay. The Hussars reported the road to be narrow but still suitable for both wheels and tracks. The route was to be Jérusalem–St-Paul-du-Vernay–Ste-Honorine-de-Ducy–Briquessard–Villers-Bocage.

A good start was made at 1600 hours and satisfactory progress was achieved until the leading troops from 8th Hussars 'bumped' a German anti-tank gun with infantry support at Livry, just north-east of Caumont. According to a German source this was from Panzer Lehr Division's Escort Company. No attempt was made to switch to another route further to the west as it was felt that this would have embarrassed the Americans, while to try to move via Belle Épine–Anctoville–Villers-Bocage would merely have led to another clash. At this stage, this was not the object of the exercise and would in all probability have given away the aim of the 'right hook'. By the time the German force at Livry had been dealt with, it was 2000 hours and Brigadier Hinde decided to halt for the night. In fact it took until midnight for the column to close up and get into a leaguer off the road in the la Mulotière area. One 8th Hussars squadron pushed out to protect the left flank in the area of le Pont Mulot and made contact with some Germans.

The night was relatively free of incident apart from some 'liberation' celebrations by the population in Livry. At 0530 hours on 13 June, the advance towards Villers-Bocage was resumed. At 0615 hours, the head of 131st Infantry Brigade reached la Paumière, where 22nd Armoured Brigade's tactical headquarters was located. They were stopped there and got off

Order of March of 22nd Armoured Brigade Group
12–13 June

8th Hussars	*Lt-Col C. Goulburn*
(only for initial move until first contact)	
4th CLY Group	
Troop, A Squadron, 4th CLY	*Lt W. Garnett*
(3 x Cromwells, 1 x Firefly)	
1st Platoon, A Company, 1st Rifle Brigade	*Lt P. Coop*
(4 x half-tracks)	
Rest of A Squadron, 4th CLY	*Major P.M.R. Scott*
Lt-Col Lord Cranley (CO 4th CLY, in scout car)	
Rest of A Company, 1st Rifle Brigade	*Major J. Wright*
(half-tracks)	
Anti-tank Section, 1st Rifle Brigade	*Lt R. Butler*
(towed 6-pounders)	
Part of Reconnaissance Troop, 4th CLY	*Lt R. Ingram*
(3 x Stuarts)	
RHQ Troop, 4th CLY	
Major A. Carr (second-in-command, in Cromwell)	
Lt C. Pearce (liaison officer, in scout car)	
Lt J. Cloudsley-Thompson (RHQ Troop Leader, in Cromwell)	
Captain P. Dyas (Cromwell)	
Regimental Sergeant-Major G. Holloway (in Cromwell)	
Lt D. Colvin (Intelligence Officer, in scout car)	
Captain H. Maclean (Medical Officer, in half-track)	
Major D. Wells (OC, K Battery, 5th RHA, in Sherman OP)	
Captain P. Victory (in Cromwell OP)	
Part of Reconnaissance Troop, 4th CLY	*Captain J. Philip-Smith*
(3 x Stuarts)	
B Squadron, 4th CLY	*Major I.B. Aird*
(15 Cromwells, 4 Fireflies)	
C Squadron, 4th CLY	*Major P. McColl*
(15 Cromwells, 4 Fireflies)	
K Battery, 5th RHA	
(Sexton self-propelled 25-pounders)	
A1 Echelon	
Tactical Brigade Headquarters	
Troop, Royal Engineers	
5th RHA (less K Battery)	*Lt-Col G.P. Gregson*
1st/7th Queen's	*Lt-Col D.S. Gordon*
5th RTR	*Lt-Col C.H. Holliman*
1st Rifle Brigade (less two companies)	*Lt-Col A.G.V. Paley*
260th Anti-Tank Battery	
(M10 Achilles self-propelled 17-pounders)	

the road, while 22nd Armoured Brigade pressed on past, with the 4th CLY group leading, 8th Hussars (less two squadrons) on right flank protection, and 11th Hussars reconnoitring both flanks of the axis.

View southwards at the les Maréchaux crossroads, where the D99 crosses the D31, looking towards Livry, where the first contact was made on the evening of 12 June. The British advance stopped for the night along the line of the D9 just to the north of Livry. *(Author)*

Overnight, Brigadier Hinde had sketched out his plan for the occupation of the Villers-Bocage area, which was as follows:

- 4th CLY would occupy high ground at Point 213 north-east of Villers-Bocage.
- 1st/7th Queen's would occupy and hold the main road entries into the town, except those to the west of the church. These three roads were the responsibility of 1st Rifle Brigade (less two companies).
- 5th RTR was to hold the high ground south-west of Villers-Bocage around Maisoncelles Pelvey.
- 260th Anti-Tank Battery would be prepared to fill the gap between 4th CLY and 5th RTR.

According to German sources, the only troops in Villers-Bocage at that time were two medical companies and Panzer Lehr Division's ambulance platoon, which had established a main dressing station and a hospital there. The division's main supply route also ran through the town. This information, however, is somewhat at variance with a later report from a member of the leading troop of A Squadron, 4th CLY, who said that a civilian in Villers-Bocage told them as they passed through the next day that he had seen eight German tanks in the town on the previous evening, but that he thought they had gone elsewhere later in the night.

However, it is very doubtful whether or not any civilians had got wind of the presence of the German tanks spending the night up at Point 213 and clearly the newly-arriving British knew nothing of them. It is also highly improbable that the Germans realised that such a large British force was now poised to infiltrate their rear, although they knew that something could happen along these lines and had taken steps to bolster the all-important Panzer Lehr Division area. The headlong collision that was about to occur would thus happen almost by chance.

The stage was set and the actors were assembling.

CHAPTER 3

THE BATTLE OF VILLERS-BOCAGE

Additional orders issued to 4th CLY for the morning of 13 June were to allow a squadron of 8th Hussars to move past to the left and then for 4th CLY to proceed with all speed through Villers-Bocage and on to the high ground at Point 213. As it was obvious that there would be no time for reconnaissance, the regiment's reconnaissance vehicles (six Stuart light tanks) would travel with RHQ Troop, the order of march being unchanged from the previous day, but with the commanding officer 'swanning' in his scout car, so he was able to go up rapidly to join his leading squadron should it be necessary. Also very near the front of the column was Lieutenant Pearce, originally of the Reconnaissance Troop but since landing in Normandy attached to RHQ Troop as a liaison officer in a Humber scout car.

It was a dry, clear morning when the 22nd Armoured Brigade units set off from their overnight position, still travelling along the single divisional centre line and unable to get off the road or to carry out much reconnaissance to the flanks due to the inevitable narrow, sunken lanes, high hedgerows, ditches, small fields and patches of thick woodland of the *bocage*. The officers all felt that they were being urged along too fast. The Yeomanry commanding officer, Lieutenant-Colonel (Lt-Col) Lord Cranley, in particular, a very experienced and vigilant leader, did not like this at all, nor did A Squadron's commander, Major Peter Scott. Nevertheless, they realised how essential it was to get onto Point 213 quickly, so they pushed on.

A German patrol in a typical Normandy farmyard. Note the VW *Kubelwagen*, which used the running gear of the familiar civilian Beetle saloon. Behind it are motorcycle troops. (*J-P. Benamou, via author's collection*)

Pearce remembered halting with RHQ Troop on a forward slope just short of the town and scouring the surrounding countryside through his binoculars. He located a German eight-wheeled armoured car half hidden in an orchard on the facing slope about 600 metres away, its commander clearly watching the column. Pearce had been following close behind the regimental second-in-command's tank (Major Arthur Carr), so he shouted over to him to engage the enemy vehicle and pointed it out. Unfortunately, the turret of Carr's Cromwell was so jam-packed with kit that it could not be traversed and nothing happened. Pearce realised that dealing quickly with this contact was essential, so he broke radio silence.

Pearce called the RHQ Troop Leader, who was behind him also in a Cromwell, and gave him details of the contact, but still nothing happened. A few minutes later, Pearce watched, with some annoyance, as the armoured car slowly turned around and disappeared out of sight amid the trees of the orchard. 'I was absolutely amazed,' recalled Pearce, 'that the armoured car had not been spotted before, but even worse, that no one fired at it at any time as it was an easy target.' He was convinced that the Germans had been watching the CLY and reporting their advance and was surprised and annoyed that no one had responded to his contact report.

> **Another member of the column was Sergeant Doug Allen, of B Squadron, 4th CLY, whose troop leader had been wounded and medically evacuated on the previous day. He recalled:**
>
> 'Progress seemed to be slow and without a troop leader I managed to follow on behind my squadron leader's tank. Away from the smell of rotting animals we approached Livry without any signs of destruction, then on to the village of Briquessard where no sign of life was apparent. Slowly we came to Amayé-sur-Seulles and halted for a short while. Anticipating enemy fire and keeping observation, the neat little village could hardly be appreciated, but a few civilians had been aroused by the sounds of our traffic. We managed a quick brew just after Amayé and made for Villers where our column halted at the lower end of the main street... VB appeared to be as peaceful and deserted as the previous hamlets and villages had been. By this time we were all relaxed and it looked as though this right hook was going to be a success. It was just after 8 a.m. and I clambered down from my Cromwell to check up on things with my friend Sergeant Lockwood just behind me... '
>
> *Source:* Letter to author from Douglas Allen.

Meanwhile, the head of the column made its way through the town along the Rue Pasteur, past the town hall and on between the shops and houses without making any contact with the Germans. Some local people came out to greet the 'conquering heroes', adding to the mood of general relaxation that seemed to pervade the entire column. After negotiating a slight left-hand bend, RHQ Troop halted just short of the eastern end of the town, whilst A Squadron continued up to Point 213. Pearce recalled that Brigadier Hinde then came up in his scout car and

Villers-Bocage today, looking north-east up the Rue Pasteur towards the centre of town. *(Author)*

talked to Lt-Col Lord Cranley for a while, then drove back into the town, while Cranley motored on towards A Squadron. A message was then passed over the radio for the platoon commanders from A Company, 1st Rifle Brigade, to make their way up to Point 213 for an orders group and this was soon taking place, one of the half-tracks moving up the column, collecting them *en route*.

However, whilst this move was in progress, it was suddenly realised what a plum target the half-track full of commanders represented, so they were hastily divided between two more vehicles to continue their journey up to Point 213. The head of the column had now reached the high ground where the leading Cromwell troop commander (Lieutenant Bill Garnett) spotted a German staff car coming along the main road towards him. He engaged it with his machine gun and watched it slew across the road into a field and catch fire. The leading tanks now began to get off the road and move into suitable hull-down positions in the fields to the south of the road, while the troop and platoon commanders were still assembling for the orders group. Further down the road, the remaining half-tracks and carriers of A Company, 1st Rifle Brigade, were in the process of moving to

the side of the road to allow an easy passage for other vehicles. All seemed peaceful and, undoubtedly, the advance guard had started to relax. Indeed, some had even begun to brew up a morning 'cuppa'.

'For Christ's sake get a move on! There's a Tiger running alongside us fifty yards away!' Sergeant O'Connor of 1st Platoon, A Company, 1st Rifle Brigade, broke radio silence with this dramatic message, as the half-track he was travelling in passed the sign to Caen on the way to Point 213 and he suddenly saw the menacing shape of the massive enemy tank looming up towards him. No one really had a chance fully to take in what he had said, before all hell broke loose.

Unknown to the British, advance elements of 2nd Company, 101st Heavy SS Panzer Battalion, had arrived in the Villers-Bocage area the evening before. They had been sent to support Panzer Lehr Division, and in particular, to close any gaps on its left flank. The tanks involved were Tiger Is under the command of *SS-Obersturmführer* (Lieutenant) Michael Wittmann, already a well-known tank ace from the Russian Front where he had over 100 kills to his credit, so he represented formidable opposition.

For various reasons explained in Tour A (*page 133*) Wittmann's company was down to just three fully serviceable Tigers, but, as events would prove, in close tank-versus-tank battles against such opponents, sheer numbers counted for little. Wittmann and his company had in fact spent the night about 200 metres to the south of the main road, quite close to Point 213, near some buildings called la Cidrerie (but often known as la Ciderie in English-language accounts). The Germans had clearly recognised the importance of Point 213 and appreciated the fact that the British would probably want to capture it. However, there is no doubt that Wittmann was still very surprised to see a long British armoured column advancing out of Villers-Bocage quite so soon. Nevertheless, he reacted with the typical flair befitting a tank ace of his calibre. As his own tank was one of those that had still to reach Point 213, he jumped on board the nearest Tiger and ordered its commander into action. Unfortunately he had chosen one with engine problems, so he swiftly transferred to another, leaving its commander to tell the rest what was happening and order them to deal with the British tanks and infantry which were now massing up at Point 213. He then drove on to the main road, turned left towards the town and began his individual march of destruction. It was approximately 0900 hours on 13 June.

The reservoirs and pylon as seen from the south, which is the direction from which the Tigers would have reached Point 213. (Author)

As he began his drive westwards, the rest of his sub-unit moved in the opposite direction, as he had ordered, and soon would begin to open up on the A Squadron tanks that had left the road at Point 213, whilst Wittmann engaged those at the rear of the squadron that were still on the road. The first tank to be hit was A Squadron's rearmost Cromwell, then a Sherman Firefly some way further up the hill. The latter slewed across the road and, as befitted a tank nicknamed the 'Ronson Lighter' (as the Ronson advertising slogan put it, 'guaranteed to light first time'), immediately started burning fiercely, effectively blocking the road to Point 213 in both directions.

WITTMANN'S ATTACK,
0900 HOURS 13 JUNE

CAEN

TILLY-SUR-SEULLES

ⓐ Calvary
ⓑ Les Hauts Vents
ⓒ Cidrerie
ⓓ Point 213
ⓔ Railway line

① 3 Stuarts (4th CLY Reconnaissance Troop)
② A Company, 1st Rifle Brigade vehicles
③ Elements A Squadron, 4th CLY
④ Several A Squadron, 4th CLY Cromwells
⑤ Positions of Tigers, am 13 June (approx.)
⑥ Possible attack route by two Tigers
⑦ Wittmann's Tiger (No. 222)
⑧ Tigers of 1st Company (early afternoon)

Notes:

1. Sources on the early stages of the battle are incomplete and sometimes contradict one another. Thus, it is impossible to be certain of the route taken by Michael Wittmann's Tiger from the company's position (5) to the N 175 main road, or at what point he reached the latter. Similarly, British accounts suggest that at least some of the fire came from north of the road, not south of it. Two French accounts also suggest the presence of one Tiger – which possibly had run out of fuel – north of the road near the calvary (a), and claim that it assisted in the destruction of the Rifle Brigade vehicles nearby.

2. The aerial photograph used here was taken on 17 June. Close examination reveals a number of knocked-out vehicles, particularly along the stretch of road north-east of the calvary.

It was down this wooded track above Montbrocq that other Tiger tanks motored to attack the leading elements of the A Squadron/A Company combat group, which Wittmann had effectively isolated when he knocked out its rear elements at the start of his progress into Villers-Bocage. *(Author)*

Wittmann then began to deal with the vehicles in the column immediately behind A Squadron – namely the Rifle Brigade half-tracks and carriers, their thin armour providing little to stop the hail of fire. Fortunately most of their occupants had dismounted and were already desperately seeking cover, but the vehicle petrol tanks were swiftly ruptured under the hail of fire from the Tiger's 88-mm main gun and its coaxially-mounted heavy machine gun. As he neared the junction with the road to Tilly-sur-Seulles, Wittmann came to the end of the infantry vehicles and was faced next by the first three Stuarts of Reconnaissance Troop. The 37-mm 'pop-guns' of the Stuarts had no effect whatsoever on the Tiger, but their paper-thin armour was hard pressed to keep out even the machine-gun bullets, let alone the Tiger's main 88-mm rounds. Soon all were burning.

101st Heavy SS Panzer Battalion

Commander: *SS-Obersturmbannführer Heinz von Westernhagen*

Headquarters	
1st Company	*SS-Hauptsturmführer Rolf Möbius*
2nd Company	*SS-Obersturmführer Michael Wittmann*
3rd Company	*SS-Obersturmführer Hanno Raasch*
4th Light/Escort Company	*SS-Obersturmführer Wilhelm Spitz*
Tank Workshop Company	*SS-Obersturmführer Gottfried Klein*

2nd Company tanks available at Villers-Bocage, 13 June:

No. 211	*SS-Obersturmführer Jürgen Wessel*
No. 221	*SS-Untersturmführer Georg Hantusch*
No. 222	*SS-Unterscharführer Kurt Sowa*
No. 223	*SS-Oberscharführer Jürgen Brendt*
No. 233	*SS-Oberscharführer Georg Lötzsch*
No. 234	*SS-Unterscharführer Herbert Stief*

Charles Pearce in his scout car was next but one in the order of march, still being just behind Major Carr's Cromwell. Behind Pearce were the rest of the RHQ Troop tanks and other vehicles. He watched in horror as Lieutenant Rex Ingram's Stuart exploded in a sheet of flame only some 200 metres away. The RHQ Troop tanks were milling around trying to escape, but their Cromwells were painfully slow in reverse and it was clear to Pearce that it was only a matter of time before they were all knocked out. He therefore decided that his best plan would be to wait until the Tiger engaged the tank in front of him, then to turn his scout car around quickly whilst it was reloading and hightail it back into Villers-Bocage, contact B Squadron and try to find a Firefly, whose 17-pounder gun was about the only tank gun that would have any effect on the Tiger. Pearce recalled what happened next:

> 'The Tiger fired and knocked out Major Carr's tank which caught fire. The flash from the 88-mm was terrific with a very loud bang, then the Tiger started forward again coming closer. My driver very calmly turned the scout car round and we started back down the road to B Squadron. I must say that the Tiger was uncomfortably close when we turned round!'

Further into town around the next corner, Pearce met the other three Reconnaissance Troop light tanks, under the command of Captain John Philip-Smith, who had deployed them into good positions off the main road. Pearce explained quickly what had happened to RHQ Troop and about the approaching Tiger, then shot off on his mission to reach B Squadron.

The wrecked British column on the road to Point 213. The firepower of a Tiger, both its main 88-mm gun and its machine guns, would have made short work of these lightly armoured vehicles, which were intended more to be cross-country infantry carriers rather than vehicles from which to fight. (IWM FLM 2778)

As might have been expected the Tiger made short work of the RHQ Troop tanks and other vehicles – all that is except for Captain Pat Dyas, who had managed to get his Cromwell off the road and into a garden and was able to remain undetected. After Wittmann passed, Dyas decided to move back onto the road and follow the Tiger, hoping to shoot it up its rear, where the armour plate was thinner. Unfortunately, he would soon be in for a nasty surprise.

After dealing with the rest of the RHQ Troop tanks, then the two artillery OP (observation post) tanks, the intelligence officer's scout car, and the medical officer's half-track, Wittmann motored on past the other half of Reconnaissance Troop. His Tiger moved into the high street, which was clear of vehicles down to the Place Jeanne d'Arc where the leading troop of B Squadron was just coming into the town, led fortunately by a Sherman Firefly (commanded by Doug Allen's friend, Sergeant Stan Lockwood). Pearce had been able to pass a warning to him before motoring

WITTMANN'S ATTACK PART TWO

CHÂTEAU D'ORBOIS

TILLY-SUR-SEULLES

POINT 213

① Knocked-out M3A3 Stuart tank, Lt Ingrams, Recce Troop
② Knocked-out M3A3 Stuart tank, Recce Troop
③ Knocked-out M3A3 Stuart tank, Recce Troop
④ Knocked-out M5 half-track, 4th CLY medical officer
⑤ Knocked-out Cromwell tank, Major Carr, RHQ Troop
⑥ Knocked-out Cromwell tank, Lt Cloudsley-Thompson, RHQ Troop
⑦ Knocked-out Cromwell tank, RSM Holloway, RHQ Troop
    (modern location 64 Rue Clemenceau)
⑧ Knocked-out Sherman OP tank, Major Wells, K Battery, 5th RHA
⑨ Knocked-out Cromwell OP tank, Captain Victory, 5th RHA
⑩ Sherman Firefly tank, Sergeant Lockwood, B Squadron, 4th CLY
⑪ Position of Wittmann's Tiger when engaged by Sergeant Lockwood
⑫ Knocked-out Cromwell tank, Captain Dyas, RHQ Troop
⊕ 6-pounder anti-tank gun, Sergeant Bray, Anti-Tank Platoon,
    A Company, 1st Rifle Brigade

ⓐ Place Jeanne d'Arc
ⓑ Rue Curie
ⓒ Ferme Gueroult
ⓓ Laurent meadow
ⓔ Ferme Lemonnier
ⓕ Garage Huet
ⓖ Calvary

on to find B Squadron commander (Major I.B. 'Ibby' Aird) to tell him what had been happening.

Through the smoke and dust Lockwood saw the flash of the Tiger's gun as it fired at the OP tanks, so he fired at the flash. Lockwood was unable to tell if he had hit anything, due to the dust and flash of his own gun (see the information on the visibility problems with firing a 17-pounder Firefly on page 71). He fired again and thought he saw a strike on the front of the Tiger, but by then the visibility was very limited. However, the firing from the 17-pounder must have caused Wittmann to stop in his tracks and realise that at last here was an enemy of whom he must take some notice and that his 'morning drive into town' was coming to an end. Wisely, after firing twice at Lockwood, Wittmann ordered his driver to turn away, and set off to return to Point 213.

Close-up of one of the three Reconnaissance Troop Stuarts which Wittmann dealt with so easily. This one appears to be burnt out: note that the rubber on the tracks has completely burned away. *(IWM FLM2782)*

Thus, unfortunately for Dyas, who was still intently following his prey, instead of having the more vulnerable rear end of the Tiger to shoot at, he found himself facing the business end of the enemy tank. It was a hopeless situation, but nevertheless, he managed to get off a couple of rounds before a single 88-mm projectile literally tore his tank to pieces, blowing Dyas completely out of the turret.

Looking south-west down the Rue Georges Clemenceau. This is roughly where Wittmann destroyed the vehicles of 4th CLY's RHQ Troop. *(Henri Marie)*

Wittmann then continued along the road, past the burning British vehicles, but his luck was about to run out. Sergeant Bray, of the anti-tank gun platoon attached to A Company, 1st Rifle Brigade, had managed to rally some of his men, and to man one of the 6-pounder anti-tank guns that was still undamaged. As the Tiger approached the Tilly-sur-Seulles road junction, looming out of the smoke and dust, they fired and hit its running gear, immobilising it. It was a fortunate strike, because the 6-pounder anti-tank gun had about the same performance with standard ammunition (new discarding sabot rounds were superior) as the Cromwell's 75-mm, so it could definitely not penetrate the Tiger's thick frontal armour (and was in the process of being replaced in anti-tank gun platoons by the much more powerful towed 17-pounder). Nevertheless it stopped the Tiger dead in its tracks. After considering his situation, Wittmann decided that he would have to abandon his tank, and hope to recover it later. Therefore he put down a curtain of fire all around his position and then, taking their personal weapons, he and his crew managed to escape unscathed. They headed off on foot, making for the Panzer Lehr Division's headquarters, which was located at Château d'Orbois, some 6 km to the north of Villers-Bocage. Wittmann and his crew would reach Château d'Orbois safely, be debriefed and then get a lift back to Point 213.

The second observation post tank was Captain Paddy Victory's Cromwell. He tried to do a neutral turn, using the tank's forward gears, so as to escape more quickly, but unfortunately a large loose paving slab got jammed between the track and drive sprocket and the tank was unable to move. Wittmann knocked it out with a single shot. (*Bundesarchiv 101/738/276/25a*)

The entire battle from start to finish had lasted for under a quarter of an hour. In that time Wittmann's personal tally had been seven cruiser/medium tanks (including one Firefly), three Stuart light tanks, one Sherman OP, nine half-tracks, four carriers and two anti-tank guns. On top of this were at least a further three cruiser tanks of A Squadron, knocked out by his other tanks up at Point 213. Others were stranded, some minus crews, with the Tigers still ready to pounce on them.

This was thus the end of Wittmann's part in the first attack, although many reports, especially those initiated by Nazi propaganda, do not mention the battle with the 6-pounder anti-tank gun occurring at this stage. Instead, they maintain that Wittmann motored back unscathed to Point 213, where he immediately stocked up with more ammunition and returned to town leading more Tigers belonging to a recently-arrived follow-up company from his battalion. This was not the case.

From 4th CLY's point of view, however, things could not have been much worse. All that was left of A Squadron and

This 6-pounder anti-tank gun commanded by Sergeant Bray of A Company, 1st Rifle Brigade, was in all probability the one that immobilised Wittmann's Tiger and forced him and his crew to bale out and leave Villers-Bocage. It points down into town. Note the rear of the Caen road sign and the distant view of an abandoned car and a knocked-out Stuart tank. *(Bundesarchiv 101/7381/2751/12a)*

The Stuart seen in the photo above (Lt Ingram's *Calamity Jane II*). Here it is being closely inspected, probably for loot. *(Bundesarchiv 101/738/275/15a)*

A Company at Point 213 were nine tanks, some minus crews who had dismounted on arrival and been unable to get back inside their vehicles, plus the disorganised riflemen of A Company and, most importantly, both the squadron commander and company commander, together with 4th CLY's commanding officer in his scout car. All could expect to be annihilated by the Tiger tanks or taken prisoner, as more and more Germans would clearly soon arrive. And this is precisely what happened. Some did manage to escape – the exciting adventures of Captain Christopher Milner, second-in-command of A Company, are recounted in Tour B (*see pp. 145–8*). The fate of those left was sealed when first a unit of panzergrenadiers arrived, followed later by eight Tigers commanded by *SS-Hauptsturmführer* (Captain) Rolf Möbius. A bad day had become a complete disaster.

Another of A Squadron's Cromwells. This one tried to escape to the north and was knocked out by a shot whose entry hole is visible in the vertical plate between the driver's position and the hull-mounted Besa machine gun in its ball mounting. (*Bundesarchiv 101/494/3376/37a*)

Charles Pearce made his way back to B Squadron headquarters, where he reported to Major Aird, who was sitting on top of his tank. In Pearce's own words, Aird 'was looking quite complacent so I climbed on his tank and saluted him. I told him about RHQ, the Tiger tank and that I had seen Sgt Lockwood. He did not acknowledge me nor did he say anything.'

Pearce later said that he was puzzled by this strange behaviour, so he then explained all about the ferocious attack that was taking place on A Squadron only a kilometre or so up the road and offered to alert Aird's squadron for him, but could get no response whatsoever from Aird. 'I was absolutely at my wits' end,' Pearce says. Fortunately just then Major Peter McColl (C Squadron's commander) arrived out of the blue asking what was happening, so Pearce explained the situation to him and that he could get no response from Aird. 'Peter, in no uncertain terms, told Ibby Aird to alert and deploy B Squadron and move them off the road. To my surprise, Ibby did take action.'

A heavily camouflaged Sd Kfz 251 armoured personnel carrier driving past the knocked-out 1st Rifle Brigade vehicles. *(Bundesarchiv 101/494/3376/239)*

In his account of the Villers-Bocage battle, Charles Pearce comments further on this 'disastrous meeting', saying that he later came to the conclusion that Aird must have resented being given advice and told what was happening by a junior officer. However, to be fair, his opinion of Aird expressed at that time is certainly at variance with what appears in the divisional after-action report where the annex about the 4th CLY operations contains the words: 'Maj Aird, who had commanded the Regiment so well and calmly since the loss of the Colonel... '

One of A Squadron's Sherman Fireflies, knocked out on the road up to Point 213. Like the Cromwell AA tank featured earlier it was nicknamed *Allakeefek* by its crew. It is being inspected by souvenir hunters during the filming of the battle scene for Nazi propaganda purposes. *(Bundesarchiv 101/494/3376/30a)*

Aird was later awarded the Distinguished Service Order for his handling of the regiment during this period, an award which, in another account of the Villers-Bocage battle in the *Sharpshooter* (the CLY Association's newsletter), Charles Pearce said 'was one of the best deserved'. I have checked with other ex-members of 4th CLY who knew Major Aird, for example, ex-Sergeant Douglas Allen, who was at one time Aird's radio operator and knew him well. His opinion was that Aird was sensible, level-headed and never indecisive, and that he (Allen) had serious doubts that the events took place in the way that Charles Pearce claimed. Allen recalled: 'I have no recollection of Pearce liaising with us during the first hour of the confusion.' Sadly both Aird and Pearce are dead, so it is impossible to check further – nor is there any need to do so. Although there were undoubtedly delays in the reaction time of some of those involved, there were good reasons for them, the most pressing being the imminent arrival of an extremely powerful enemy.

British Tanks of the Villers-Bocage Battle

Cruiser Mark VIII Cromwell

Length: 6.34 m; *Width:* 3.04 m; *Height:* 2.83 m; *Weight:* 27.5 tons;
Main armament: 75-mm; *Armour:* 8–76 mm; *Crew:* 5; *Road speed:* 51 km/hr

One tank man's view of the Cromwell was as follows: 'Most of us were in Cromwells, which I still think was a useless tank, fast enough but without adequate armour and undergunned.' See also what Maj-Gen Erskine had to say as quoted on pages 32–3.

Sherman M4 series

Length: 5.89 m; *Width:* 2.67 m; *Height:* 2.74 m; *Weight:* 30+ tons;
Main armament: 75-mm; *Armour:* 12–75 mm; *Crew:* 5; *Road speed:* 46 km/hr

The Sherman was of course designed and manufactured in the USA, and was the most widely used tank of the war, 49,234 being built. They were used by US and British forces from 1942 onwards. The Sherman was mechanically very reliable and had good mobility but by 1944 both its firepower and protection were inadequate to cope with the latest German tanks.

Sherman Firefly (Mark IVC and VC)

Length: 6.27 m (with gun); *Width:* 2.67 m; *Height:* 2.74 m; *Weight:* 34 tons;
Main armament: 17-pounder (76-mm); *Armour:* 12–75 mm; *Crew:* 4;
Road speed: 40.2 km/hr

In a bid to correct the limited firepower of the standard Sherman, British designers modified the turret to accept a version of the 17-pounder anti-tank gun. This was much more powerful than the 75-mm previously fitted but its greater size also caused difficulties.

The all-important rate of fire on the Firefly was slow, because a complex procedure had to be followed: the loader/radio operator cradled the long (0.76 m/2.5 ft) shell in both arms to edge it into the breech, tapping the commander's legs when ready. The gunner would have his sights on the target after receiving an estimated range and the commander would then give a preliminary warning over the crew intercom system: '3-2-1-fire!' giving the crew time to clap their hands over their earphones, close their eyes and open their mouths, so as to absorb the massive shockwave inside the tank. With a muzzle velocity of some 880 m/sec the armour piercing shot had travelled 1,000 metres before the flash died away, so it was impossible to observe a hit/miss on any target under that range – only the after effects. The tank recoiled almost a foot every time the gun fired, so the gunner had immediately to relay onto the target before the process was repeated, so the rate of fire was slow – but the results well worth waiting for. It was capable of penetrating 130 mm of armour at 1,000 metres.

Stuart Mark VI (M5 & M5A1)

Length: 4.34 m; *Width:* 2.23 m; *Height:* 2.31 m; *Weight:* 15 tons;
Main armament: 37-mm; *Armour:* 12–67 mm; *Crew:* 4; *Road speed:* 58 km/hr

Successor to the previous American M3 series light tank, the 'Honey' was much liked by its crews, but could no longer be considered as anything other than a reconnaissance vehicle, lacking in both firepower and protection.

HISTORY

These members of the 4th CLY advance guard were captured on 13 June mainly around Point 213. Lt-Col Lord Cranley is not among them as he managed to evade capture until the following day. *(Bundesarchiv 101/720/303/24)*

A temporary regimental headquarters was then set up with Major Aird as acting commanding officer, as he was senior to Peter McColl. Communications were established with tactical brigade headquarters at Amayé-sur-Seulles, who said that B Squadron should try to break through and link up with the beleaguered A Squadron. This was going to be extremely difficult, not just because of the fighting still going on in Villers-Bocage and at Point 213. Although A Squadron and A Company survivors at Point 213 had started to recover from the initial shock of the Tigers' devastating attack, and Lt-Col Lord Cranley was manfully trying to establish a defensive position, many of the soldiers – both infantry and tank crews – were still taking cover in the ditches and hedgerows, not unnaturally bent on trying to escape from the German tank and small-arms fire, rather than forming a cohesive defence.

To make matters worse, the first new arrivals at Point 213 that morning were panzergrenadiers from 4th Light Company of 101st Heavy SS Panzer Battalion, tipping the odds even further in the Germans' favour. They rapidly began winkling out, then collecting and marshalling together, the remnants of the 4th CLY advance guard, so that all thoughts of a successful defence were swiftly overtaken by events. By 1030 hours the position had become completely untenable and just before 1100 hours, the commanding officer's scout car and all the A Squadron radios went off the air and were not heard from again. This news was passed on to brigade headquarters and Brigadier Hinde ordered B Squadron to hold Villers-Bocage at all costs. The tanks of B Squadron would soon be joined by those of C Squadron and elements of 1st/7th Queen's, which had now also begun to arrive at the western approaches around Place Jeanne d'Arc.

Rue Pasteur, from the town hall square. Wittmann's Tiger was knocked out in this street. *(Henri Marie)*

Lt-Col Desmond Gordon, commanding officer of 1st/7th Queen's, allocated areas of the little town to his companies. He put A Company in the area of the railway station (the rail line has been removed since the war) and both B and C along the main street and covering the eastern entrances to the town. His infantrymen went into the houses, shops and gardens, installing their machine guns, mortars, PIATs and anti-tank guns in suitable positions to fire out of doors and windows, covering alleyways, roads and squares. Then they waited for the Germans to arrive.

They did not have long to wait as GenLt Bayerlein's Panzer Lehr Division was now fully alerted to the incursions to its south-west and had already begun to assemble a force to protect its rear. *Major* Helmut Ritgen helped to collect every available tank (a total of about 15 Panzer IVs) and was sent to seal off the exits out of Villers-Bocage to the west and north, but soon ran into a screen of anti-tank guns, which he rightly assumed was part of the British all-round defence of Villers-Bocage.

Meanwhile, Michael Wittmann and his crew had reached GenLt Bayerlein's headquarters at Château d'Orbois and had been debriefed. They were then given transport so that they could make their way back to Point 213 to rejoin what was left of their company. However, by the time they got there a second Tiger company had also arrived: this was SS-Captain Rolf Möbius' 1st Company, 101st Heavy SS Panzer Battalion. Möbius had some eight fit Tigers with him. Clearly, as Wittmann had the most up-to-date information on the British defences in Villers-Bocage, he would have briefed Möbius on what had happened and where the British were located. There is some divergence, however, in the accounts of what Wittmann did next (*see Tour B, page 149*). Suffice it to say that a strong German force of tanks and panzergrenadiers was formed, including both *Waffen-SS* and Panzer Lehr Division troops, but not including Wittmann, which then re-entered the town from the north and north-east. The fighting in Villers-Bocage was far from over.

LIEUTENANT COTTON'S AMBUSH

Prior to this German advance, and having been unable to make any progress up the main road towards A Squadron, Major Aird had sent out his 4th Troop (commanded by Lieutenant Bill Cotton) to try to find another route around the town to the south so as to get to Point 213 that way. This was unsuccessful and Cotton soon returned to the centre of the town, ending up in the town hall square. Further movement towards the north-east was now becoming increasingly dangerous and unmistakable track noises of heavy German armour could be heard (either the Möbius Tigers or the Panzer Lehr Panzer IVs – or both). Wisely, Cotton stopped in the town hall square and swiftly set up an ambush with his troop, which included a Sherman Firefly. He was also supported by a 6-pounder anti-tank gun belonging to 1st/7th Queen's and some of the battalion's infantrymen armed with PIATs.

Battle was soon joined with both sides scoring kills. Up to six Tigers and three Panzer IVs (sources differ) were knocked out in

VILLERS-BOCAGE – AFTERNOON, 13 JUNE

① Approximate route followed by Cotton's troop
② Ambush position of Cotton's troop
③ Elements Panzer Lehr Division, pm 13 June
④ Elements 1st Company, 101st Heavy SS Panzer
   Battalion and Panzer Lehr Division, pm 13 June

◑ Knocked-out Tiger
✚ Knocked-out Panzer IV
◎ Cromwell
● Sherman Firefly
⊕ 6-pdr anti-tank gun

ⓐ Place Jeanne d'Arc
ⓑ Rue Saint-Germain
ⓒ Rue Emile Samson
ⓓ Boulevard Joffre
ⓔ Place du Marché
ⓕ Railway station
ⓖ Rue Pasteur
ⓗ Railway (embanked)

CHÂTEAU
DE VILLERS
500 metres

and around the town by anti-tank gun and PIAT fire and Cotton's ambush (*for details see Tour B, pp. 151–8*). This deadly game of 'cat and mouse' went on for some six hours in the narrow streets, squares and alleyways of Villers-Bocage.

Two panzergrenadiers, their MP 40s slung after the fighting had ended, stroll down the main street in Villers-Bocage past one of the knocked-out Tigers. *(Bundesarchiv 101/738/276/30a)*

Villers-Bocage was still in British hands at 1600 hours when the Germans put in yet another determined attack, supported by mortar and heavy artillery fire. The attack was held, but the close street fighting continued, with small groups of German infantrymen working their way through the scattered British positions. At the railway station, A Company was overwhelmed and a complete platoon taken prisoner, whilst in another part of town the 1st/7th Queen's battalion headquarters was virtually surrounded.

As the pressure mounted, Brigadier Hinde reluctantly decided that the situation was becoming untenable and that 22nd Armoured Brigade must be withdrawn from Villers-Bocage to a more secure area, where it could spend the night in a small, well protected 'brigade box' rather than in narrow, winding town streets. The plan was for the infantry to withdraw first, with B and C Squadrons, 4th CLY, covering their rear. This was achieved, the withdrawal being greatly assisted by a diversionary shoot by K Battery, 5th Royal Horse Artillery (RHA), onto the town, including an extremely accurate smoke screen. 5th RTR took up positions guarding all the approaches to the withdrawal route as the column fought its way slowly back to 'The Island Position' (so-called in 22nd Armoured Brigade's after-action report) to the east of Amayé-sur-Seulles. The next, critical phase of the operation was now about to begin.

Brigadier Hinde had this to say about the last phase of the battle in Villers-Bocage:

'The performance of 1/7 Queen's and two squadrons of 4 Sharpshooters [4th CLY] in holding the town until ordered to withdraw was deserving of high praise and the action of the tanks in covering the withdrawal of the infantry was admirably executed in very difficult circumstances.'

Source: Report by commander 22nd Armoured Brigade.

Panzergrenadiers outside Bijoux FIX (a jeweller's shop) in Villers-Bocage. Looting from civilian shops or houses was punished severely, so it is doubtful if they actually tried to 'liberate' anything despite the damage giving them easy access. *(Bundesarchiv 101/738/276/31a)*

HISTORY

Of course this had not been achieved without considerable loss of both men and vehicles. The total of casualties for 13–14 June was some 378 killed, wounded and taken prisoner, broken down as follows:

4th CLY: 15 officers (including the commanding officer, second-in-command, A Squadron's officer commanding, the adjutant and the medical officer) and 86 other ranks
1st Rifle Brigade: 4 officers and 145 other ranks
1st/7th Queen's: 8 officers and 120 other ranks
22nd Armoured Brigade lost some 27 tanks (20 Cromwells, 4 Fireflies and 3 Stuarts) and 28 other armoured fighting vehicles, plus other light tanks and armoured cars from the reconnaissance regiments.

CHAPTER 4

THE BATTLE OF THE ISLAND POSITION

The Island Position was none too large for the mass of transport, tanks and guns inside. However, every available infantryman was needed as the frontages to cover were very long. The Queen's Regiment history records, for example, that every single man in 1st/5th Queen's was employed in the front line apart from the commanding officer, the second-in-command, the intelligence officer and one signaller who manned battalion headquarters. The British force was now up against not only the tanks and panzergrenadiers of Panzer Lehr Division and the *Waffen-SS*, but also 2nd Panzer Division, which was arriving from the south.

Brigadier Hinde recorded the establishment of the Island Position:

'In consultation with Comd 131 Bde, I now organised a defensive perimeter for the night with 1/5 Queen's astride the road east of Amayé-sur-Seulles and including St-Germain, 1/7 Queen's completing the "box" east of 1/5 Queen's, also astride the road; one motor company of 1 RB [1st Rifle Brigade] was also used to fill a gap between 1/5 and 1/7 Queen's south of the road. At last light the armour and anti-tank guns were all drawn within the infantry dispositions. During the evening, enemy infantry mainly south of the road, confined their activities to patrolling and sniping; enemy shelling was negligible. I much appreciate the help of Brig Ekins (comd 131 Queen's Bde) in arranging the dispositions of his two battalions.'

Source: Report by commander 22nd Armoured Brigade.

Amayé-sur-Seulles on the D71. *En route* for Villers-Bocage on the morning of 13 June, the British column would not have paid much heed to the little village as it pushed on towards its objective. However, it would assume considerably more importance later that day, when the survivors of the battle withdrew into the nearby 'Island Position'. *(Author)*

The night of 13/14 June passed quietly enough, 1st/7th Queen's spending a virtually incident-free night in its position facing towards Villers-Bocage, for instance. No one was able to relax, of course, despite being exhausted after a long day of fighting. At first light, 5th RTR moved its tanks up into the fighting positions they had occupied during the previous day. Brigadier Hinde then made a tour of the defences to make sure they were strong everywhere, while the infantry battalions sent out reconnaissance patrols to check on German locations. They soon reported that there were Germans in Bruyère, Tracy-Bocage and le Haut de St-Louet, which gives a graphic impression of how close the Germans were to the perimeter. Amayé-sur-Seulles

HISTORY

was clear and so it was immediately occupied by a standing patrol.

A member of 4th CLY who was in the Island Position wrote:

'We were now completely surrounded… firing went on everywhere, also considerable sniping. 1st RTR kept the road open behind us but only just managed it. We were attacked all the next day. In the evening a very big attack was put in against us, but we held them.'

Source: Extract from article 'The First 70 Days in Normandy', published in *The Sharpshooter.*

Heavy and accurate Allied artillery fire helped to keep the brigade box near Amayé-sur-Seulles intact during 14 June. Fire from weapons like this 5.5-inch gun belonging to 64th Medium Regiment, Royal Artillery, of 50th Infantry Division, were ideal for giving such support. They had a range of 20,500 metres and a shell weight of 25 kg. *(IWM B5452)*

He goes on to explain that they were greatly aided by American 155-mm gunners and RAF rocket-firing Typhoons. Another eyewitness (in 1st Rifle Brigade) bemoaned the fact that

THE ISLAND POSITION, 13–14 JUNE

① Carriers, 1st/5th Queen's
② A Company, 1st/5th Queens
③ B Company, 1st/5th Queen's
④ C Company, 1st/5th Queen's
⑤ D Company, 1st/5th Queen's
⑥ Carriers, 1st/7th Queen's
⑦ A Company, 1st/7th Queen's
⑧ B Company, 1st/7th Queen's
⑨ C Company, 1st/7th Queens
⑩ D Company, 1st/7th Queen's
⑪ Platoon, 1st Rifle Brigade
⑫ C Company, 1st Rifle Brigade
⑬ Carriers, 1st Rifle Brigade
⑭ Elements 1st Rifle Brigade
⑮ 8th and 11th Hussars
⑯ C Battery, 5th RHA
⑰ G Battery, 5th RHA
⑱ K Battery, 5th RHA

● Tactical headquarters, 22nd Armoured Brigade
●▶ Gun of 260th Anti-Tank Battery (showing direction of fire)

Base map: IGN 1513O

NOTE

5th RTR was deployed on the northern edge and at the eastern end of the island, with B Squadron supporting the 1st Rifle Brigade elements at la Commune (numbered 11) and A Squadron with B and C Companies, 1st/7th Queen's. C Squadron was deployed in support of the latter's A and D Companies with a troop patrolling the gap between the 1st Rifle Brigade troops to the west (numbered 14). 4th CLY occupied positions in and around St-Germain.

Metres

0   250   500

the position was too constricted to allow for proper tactical dispersal for the number of vehicles it contained, so casualties were higher than might otherwise have been expected. A further eyewitness (in 1st/7th Queen's) said that the main problem was that fields of fire were restricted to about 50 to 200 metres, whilst the Germans occupied the high ground on three sides of the position.

All without exception praised the artillery support and it is clear from all the eye-witnesses that it was the close, accurate artillery fire, which saved the position time and time again. In addition to 5th RHA, the units of 22nd Armoured Brigade were able to call upon support from 3rd RHA, 5th Army Group Royal Artillery, and the artillery of 1st US Infantry Division. With 5th RHA there was also a battery captain from 64th Medium Regiment and two from 52nd Heavy Regiment, so the links to a range of available firepower were considerable. During the next 36 hours many calls for prompt and accurate fire were made and answered with the minimum of delay. The tour map on page 144 shows the major targets engaged during 14 June, but it was the tremendous volume of fire achieved that evening which was probably the most significant and important.

During the morning of 14 June the divisional centre line back to Briquessard was again opened and kept secure by 1st RTR and 1st/6th Queen's (as already mentioned by one of the eye-witnesses). Maj-Gen Erskine visited the Island Position at about 1000 hours and at 1600 hours Brigadier Hinde attended a conference at 131st Infantry Brigade's tactical headquarters, at which the divisional commander gave out orders.

The gist of these orders was that, owing to the slow progress made by 50th Infantry Division around Tilly-sur-Seulles and the consequent vulnerability of the 7th Armoured Division, 22nd Armoured Brigade would have to be withdrawn during the night

Looking south-east from St-Germain towards Villers-Bocage. From here one can try to locate some of the targets engaged by artillery as shown on the map on page 144, to give an idea of how closely the action was fought. Unfortunately, this is rather difficult, as the field system has changed so much. *(Author)*

The British force also enlisted the help of US Army artillery from US V Corps, whose 155-mm guns laid down excellent supporting fire from positions north of Caumont-l'Éventé. *(IWM B5404)*

Gunners in action. The ubiquitous 25-pounders of the Royal Artillery saw service worldwide. Here a pair of 25-pounder Mark IIs are seen in action in the Tilly-sur-Seulles area on 17 June. They belong to 386th Battery of 185th Field Regiment, 49th Infantry Division. *(IWM B5664)*

of 14/15 June. The division would then take up defensive positions between the Americans and the right flank of 50th Infantry Division, with 131st Infantry Brigade on the right and 22nd Armoured Brigade on the left of the new divisional area.

Meanwhile a relatively quiet morning had been shattered completely at about 1100 hours when a determined attack was mounted against C Company, 1st/7th Queen's, the battalion's left forward company. A violent small-arms battle erupted. One platoon that was sited in front of the others was overrun, but the rest of the company counter-attacked with Stens and grenades and restored the situation. The Germans quietened down, then became more active in the afternoon, firstly from the direction of Villers-Bocage and then le Haut de St-Louet, another attack being put in on 1st/7th Queen's at about 1400 hours, which caused some casualties. The major German offensive did not begin until about 1900 hours, however, when a two-pronged assault started, one prong being on to the southern perimeter, the other on the north-eastern side.

German Tanks of the Villers-Bocage Battle

Panzer IV Ausführung H

Length: 5.91 m (6.63 m with gun overhang); *Width:* 2.92 m; *Height:* 2.59 m; *Weight:* 25 tons; *Main armament:* 75-mm KwK 40/L48; *Armour:* 10–80 mm; *Crew:* 5; *Road speed:* 40 km/hr

The backbone of the German armoured forces, the Panzer IV was in full production before 1939 and still in full production in 1944 (in greatly updated versions; *Ausführung H* translates roughly as 'Mark H'), its turret ring being big enough to accept larger, more powerful guns, whilst its protection and mobility had also been constantly improved. Its high velocity 75-mm gun made it a powerful opponent.

Panzer V Panther, Ausführung A

Length: 6.68m (8.86 m with gun overhang); *Width:* 3.43 m; *Height:* 2.97 m; *Weight:* 44.8 tons; *Main armament:* 75-mm KwK 42/L70; *Armour:* 16–110 mm; *Crew:* 5; *Road speed:* 54.7 km/hr

Designed to restore the balance after the powerful Russian T-34 had made its appearance on the battlefield. Classed as a heavy medium tank, the Panther was an excellent armoured fighting vehicle in most respects, its gun being able to knock out a Sherman at 1,000 metres head on, or at 2,800 metres side and rear.

Panzer VI Tiger, Ausführung E

Length: 7.25m (8.45 m with gun overhang); *Width:* 3.56 m; *Height:* 3 m; *Weight:* 57 tons; *Main armament:* 88-mm KwK 36/L56; *Armour:* 25–110 mm; *Crew:* 5; *Road speed:* 37 km/hr

The fearsome reputation gained by the relatively small number of Tigers built (just over 1,300 Tiger Is and 489 Tiger IIs) was due to their outstanding armament and protection rather than mechanical reliability. The KwK 36 gun was a parallel development to the standard FlaK 18 and could defeat 119 mm of armour at 1,000 metres and 90 mm at 2,500 metres – so one can imagine the effect of it firing at any of the Allied armoured fighting vehicles then in service at ranges out to 2,500 metres.

G Battery, 5th RHA, was almost immediately in the closest action possible, engaging German infantry over open sights with airburst ammunition at under 400 metres. K Battery fired to the east in support of 1st/7th Queen's, whilst C Battery fired to the south at a range of 700 metres onto the main assault, expending some 1,400 rounds in just three hours. It was a bitter, unrelenting battle. In one area, three companies of infantry, each supported by three Tiger tanks, almost broke through but were stopped by the crushing artillery fire. 700–800 casualties were believed to have been inflicted on the Germans in these attacks and at least eight German tanks were destroyed.

HISTORY

Men of 1st Rifle Brigade, 22nd Armoured Brigade, searching captured Germans. The badge the prisoners wear on their arms depicts the *Edelweiss* flower, denoting that they are mountain troops. *(IWM B5517)*

Fighting died down at about 2200 hours and some two and a half hours later, the withdrawal from the Island Position began. The order of march along the divisional centre line was: 1st/5th Queen's; 4th CLY; 1st/7th Queen's (less one company); 5th RHA; brigade headquarters; troop of Royal Engineers; 260th Anti-Tank Battery; 1st Rifle Brigade (less one company), 8th Hussars (less one squadron); 11th Hussars; and lastly the rearguard.

The rearguard comprised 5th RTR, plus the companies from 1st Rifle Brigade and 1st/7th Queen's, a squadron from 8th Hussars and detachments of 1st/5th Queen's, all under the command of Lt-Col C.H. Holliman, commanding officer of 5th RTR. The start point was St-Germain. As the move began, the RAF bombed Aunay-sur-Odon, providing excellent noise cover, whilst an artillery harassing programme to both north and south of the withdrawal route also helped cover the noise of the tank tracks.

The Germans were, on the whole, slow to realise that the position was being evacuated and the entire force got away without any major incidents. 2nd Panzer Division was especially slow in reacting to the withdrawal. Just one tank ditched across the road to form a roadblock, with even a small, determined force covering such a blockage, would undoubtedly have caused chaos in the British column and allowed 2nd Panzer Division to deal effectively with the entire armoured brigade at first light. Instead the brigade was allowed to escape and 'lived to fight another day'. One can imagine the relief of all concerned when they finally reached their new positions, safely back behind friendly forward defensive locations.

The 4th CLY history encapsulated this final scene:

'The artillery were laying a concentration in the direction of Villers and, as it grew dark, Lancasters came over to drop their bombs, the noise of their engines drowning the sounds of the withdrawal which went like clockwork. The Sharpshooters were in leaguer at 0400 hrs and everybody, dead tired, was asleep within a few minutes.'

Source: Andrew Graham, *Sharpshooters at War.*

So ended Operation Perch and the daring 'right hook' action to break out of the beachhead area. It had failed primarily because of the bravery and expertise of a single tank commander, SS-Lieutenant Michael Wittmann, who would be awarded the Swords to his Knight's Cross for his valour. The citation stated that by 14 June 1944, he had knocked out a staggering 138 tanks and 132 anti-tank guns in his relatively short career. As we have also seen, the Desert Rats had more than made up for their lack of vigilance at Villers-Bocage on 13 June. It would, however, be almost two more months before British troops would re-enter the shattered little market town, which would be bombed almost flat later in the month.

Although perhaps overshadowed by what had gone before, the events of 13 and 14 June are undoubtedly memorable. The anti-tank guns of 1st/7th Queen's alone knocked out four Tiger tanks and shared two more kills with 4th CLY. In addition two more Tigers were damaged by infantry tank-hunting parties. The myth of the Tiger's invincibility had certainly been severely dented, if not proved to be false. All the infantry battalions in 7th Armoured Division had now experienced their first heavy German attacks and had driven them back at considerable cost to

HISTORY

the enemy. In his report on the action, the commander of 1st/7th Queen's, Lt-Col Gordon, commented: 'The result of that has shown that if every soldier stands firm and fights hard with all his weapons he has nothing to fear from the Hun.'

CHAPTER 5

50TH INFANTRY DIVISION: LINGÈVRES AND LES VERRIÈRES

As we have seen, 7th Armoured Division's 'right hook' had ended in failure and the division was now virtually back where it had started, having suffered heavy casualties in both men and matériel. However, the operation had not been a complete disaster – the losses, though heavy, could be replaced. Equally heavy casualties had been inflicted on the Germans during the battles for Villers-Bocage and around the Island Position. Precious tanks and panzergrenadiers had been lost and the Germans would find it hard to replace them. The pressure further to the west, where the Americans would make their break-out, had been lessened by the fact that German armour had had to be diverted to the eastern end of the beachhead, in line with Monty's intended and oft-stated aim.

Nevertheless, progress on the 50th Infantry Division front had also been minimal up to 13 June. The 'curse of the *bocage*' retained its grip and Tilly-sur-Seulles and the surrounding area remained in German hands. However, 49th (West Riding) Infantry Division had now come into the line to the east of 50th Infantry Division, allowing the 'Tyne Tees' Division to concentrate on the Tilly-sur-Seulles, Hottot-les-Bagues and Belle Épine area. The immediate objective was the road (now the D9) running south-west through Juvigny, south of Tilly-sur-Seulles.

On 14 June, whilst 7th Armoured Division was fighting for the Island Position, 50th Infantry Division launched a divisional attack with two brigades (151st and 231st) supported by RAF fighter ground attack and the full divisional artillery. 151st

LINGÈVRES, 14 JUNE

① C and D Companies, 9th DLI
② A and B Companies, 9th DLI
③ Major Mogg's headquarters
④ One platoon, C Company, 9th DLI
⑤ Two platoons, D Company, 9th DLI
⑥ 9th DLI anti-tank guns
◑ Sergeant Harris' first position
● Corporal Johnson's tank destroyed
○ Sergeant Harris' second position
● Knocked-out Panthers

Base map: IGN 1512OT

0   100   200
Metres

91

D 33a

rtinière

C

③

Bérolles

82

les Verrières

la Senaudière

Éc.

200 metres

⑤

⑥

90

④

0,5

C

Lingèvres

Longraye

Lieu Meslier

94

(Durham) Infantry Brigade, comprising 6th, 8th and 9th DLI, supported by the tanks of 4th/7th Dragoon Guards, began the assault by launching 9th DLI to capture the village of Lingèvres, some 3 km west of Tilly-sur-Seulles. 6th DLI was to attack the neighbouring hamlet of les Verrières to the north-east (simply called 'Verrières' in 1944). If this latter attack was successful, 6th DLI would then push on southwards towards Hottot-les-Bagues. Both attacks pitted the Geordies against the extremely skilled panzergrenadiers of Panzer Lehr Division, who could be expected to make the fullest use of the very difficult *bocage* country, where surprise was very easy to achieve and death lurked around every corner.

Lt-Col Humphrey Wood, 9th DLI's commanding officer, had made his feelings very clear at the brigade orders group on the afternoon of 13 June, when he said that the attack should be carried out at night and that time should be allowed for a full and careful reconnaissance. Unfortunately, as the brigadier pointed out, speed was of the essence because of the vital need to break out from the beachhead as quickly as possible, the programme for which was now falling well behind schedule. It was agreed, however, that 9th DLI should conduct a 'reconnaissance in force' that evening. This was undertaken by

Corps commander's conference. Lt-Gen Gerry Bucknall, holding a conference in the field on 13 June. Those with him include GOC 50th Infantry Division, Maj-Gen Douglas Graham (at rear without a hat) and GOC 49th Infantry Division, Maj-Gen E.H. Barker (on right of Bucknall, sitting on ground). *(IWM B5510)*

B Company, supported by the carrier platoon, with artillery support on call via a forward observation officer. This suffered severe losses, as explained in Tour C (*pp. 162–4*)

The main attack was scheduled to start at 1015 hours on 14 June, with both battalions advancing southwards, 9th DLI first into Lingèvres, then 6th DLI into les Verrières, preceded by artillery barrages and ground attack air strikes.

The Germans were occupying a large wood which lay astride 9th DLI's axis of advance and was situated only a few hundred metres in front of its forming up-positions. A and C Companies were to attack the wood after it had been hit by concentrated artillery fire and rocket-firing Typhoons.

> **The barrage seemed overwhelming but Sergeant Charles Eagles of 9th DLI recalled what followed:**
>
> 'For what seemed a long time nothing happened and then an enemy tank in the left hand corner fired and set fire to one of our Shermans. The fire was returned with good effect by the other two.'
>
> *Source:* Quoted in Harry Moses, *The Gateshead Gurkhas.*

Another German tank began to fire at the supporting tanks and then the entire wood came to life. The leading infantry were now in the middle of the stubble and were caught in withering machine-gun and sniper fire. There was nothing for it but to continue the dash into the wood. By now A Company on the left had suffered heavy casualties, including all its officers. Lt-Col Wood decided to order the two reserve companies to move up straight away, B to pass through A, whilst D closed up to support C on the right. They managed to get through the wood and into the village, but sustained more heavy casualties, including Lt-Col Wood, who was wounded by a mortar bomb and died almost immediately. His place was taken by Major John Mogg, late of the Oxfordshire and Buckinghamshire Light Infantry, who had joined the battalion as second-in-command just before the invasion.

Mogg immediately took firm control and, despite the heavy casualties it had sustained, 9th DLI captured the village and drove out the defenders. Mogg then took stock of his resources and set about organising the defence of the village. He also called his support weapons forward, but positioned his anti-tank guns

HISTORY

badly and, during the first German counter-attack, four out of the five were knocked out. Luckily, however, the battalion still had the close support of A Squadron, 4th/7th Dragoon Guards, which played a vital role in the defence.

4th/7th Dragoon Guards' war diary explained that the regiment:

'... had a wonderful day, knocking out six Panthers, one anti-tank gun and one half-track and capturing intact one 'Peoples Car' [*Kübelwagen*] and one half-track that was brought back for use in the Regt... It was a great sight to see all these enemy Panthers burning in a row.'

Source: War Diary 4th/7th RDG, Tank Museum.

Most of this mayhem was caused, as in the Villers-Bocage battle, by a single tank crew. This time it was that of a Sherman Firefly, commanded by Sergeant Wilf Harris (*see Tour C, pp. 167–76*). Initially he had observed tank movement to the east of the village, about 1,000 metres away. It appeared to be a Sherman (captured?) and, as Harris watched it through his binoculars, it stopped about 800 metres away and two Panthers pulled out from behind it and began to advance towards the village. Harris destroyed the first and hit the second and stopped it. It was later finished off by an infantry tank-hunting party.

At about 1230 hours, another German tank was seen coming from the direction of Tilly. Harris fired at it as it passed in front of the previous Panther (now 'dead'), and it caught fire immediately. He then moved his position nearer the church in the centre of the village where the troop corporal's tank was located. The corporal then observed a further German tank in the same area as the others. Neither tank could engage the newcomer properly, but it started to drop high explosive ammunition onto the buildings near to the troop corporal's tank, so he then went forward to where he could see better. The two tanks then fired at each other simultaneously. The Sherman was badly hit and all the crew except one were killed or wounded. The German vehicle then withdrew, leaving the village still in the hands of 9th DLI and its supporting tanks. Sergeant Harris moved his position to the west side of the village.

At about 1615 hours, the firing began again and the threat of another tank attack was again apparent, but this time from the

The fourth of the Panthers to be knocked out by Sergeant Harris standing beside the village war memorial in Lingèvres. *(IWM B5781)*

The Lingèvres war memorial today. *(Author)*

west. German tanks were spotted some distance away and engaged, one being set on fire and knocked out. This provoked the remaining Panthers into advancing into the village where, as described in Stand C4 *(pp. 173–6)*, three more were knocked out.

HISTORY

This is a PIAT (Projector Infantry Anti-Tank), the hand-held anti-tank weapon used by the infantry tank-hunting parties at Lingèvres. *(IWM B8913)*

In all, nine German tanks were put out of action or destroyed during the day by the Durham Light Infantry anti-tank guns and their tank support, a considerable feat when one remembers that the Germans had far superior tanks in all respects except for the firepower of the lone Firefly.

Thus, despite continual pressure, 9th DLI held the village and established contact with 6th DLI on the left in les Verrières and 231st Infantry Brigade on the right. That evening 9th DLI was relieved by 2nd Glosters of 56th Infantry Brigade. The Durhams' losses had been considerable: out of a complement of some 590 all ranks, they had lost 22 officers and 226 other ranks killed, wounded and missing.

On the left flank of the 'Gateshead Gurkhas' another Geordie battalion, 6th DLI, was faced with much the same situation. H-Hour for it was slightly later than it was for 9th DLI, meaning it could receive the same artillery and close air support, which first hammered the woods in front of the hamlet of les Verrières. No-man's-land between the two sets of forward defensive locations was very similar, comprising cornfields and woods. The Geordies crossed the open ground in front of the woods in much

The late General Sir John Mogg, GCB, CBE, DSO, in later life as Deputy Supreme Allied Commander NATO. Mogg was promoted and awarded the Distinguished Service Order for his part in the Lingèvres action. *(Author's collection)*

the same way as 9th DLI had done, in extended line with two companies up (C and D), supported by a squadron of 4th/7th Dragoon Guards.

Here, too, the Germans, who were dug in along the forward edge of the wood line, held their fire until the leading troops were within some 150 metres, then a dozen machine guns opened fire. For a while the attackers were halted, but they managed to battle on, finally entering the wood, which took until mid-afternoon to clear. The depleted battalion then paused along the line of the German positions in the woods to reorganise, before pressing on to take the hamlet. The Germans had left behind some of their machine guns, a large quantity of ammunition, some 75-mm guns and even two of their half-tracks, all of which were used against them in this final assault.

However, although the Geordies successfully took les Verrières, they were then held up by strong resistance beyond the straggle of houses and farms and could get no further south than about 200 metres from the Tilly–Lingèvres road. That night they withdrew just to the north of les Verrières itself and prepared for a further advance on 15 June. They had lost just over 100 killed, wounded and missing, plus some 17 crewmen from the five knocked-out tanks of B Squadron, 4th/7th Dragoon Guards, which, like A Squadron, had played a tremendous part in the attack. One officer of 6th DLI said, 'Tanks crashed through hedges, shooting into hedge junctions and giving magnificent support.'

He went on to say that this had been by far the most successful attack that the battalion carried out during six days of heavy and continuous fighting. It undoubtedly showed what could be done when infantry, tanks and artillery all worked in perfect

Looking southwards towards les Verrières from the position of the British forward defensive locations to the north. Buildings can be made out among the trees but, as for Lingèvres, the corn was standing nearer the hamlet than in this photograph. As on the other flank, the Germans had cut a 'killing zone' in the corn near the tree line. *(Author)*

co-operation, and after a number of not too successful attempts they seemed to have hit upon the best method of achieving success. And this victory had a morale-boosting effect.

The Durham Light Infantry regimental history recalls:

'The weary look in the eyes of the men was once again replaced by keenness and eagerness, and even after six days of fighting the defences in our new positions were dug more quickly and better than ever.'

Source: Harry Moses, *The Gateshead Gurkhas.*

The following day, 2nd Essex of 56th Infantry Brigade completed the capture of Tilly-sur-Seulles, meeting little opposition. The little town had, like Villers-Bocage, been battered and bombed almost beyond all recognition – what a price its citizens had had to pay for liberation. Their understanding and fortitude undoubtedly won the sympathy and respect of all those who had been forced to inflict the damage in order to free them from the Nazis.

One of the casualties at les Verrières was Major 'Spike' Galloway of 6th DLI, who was wounded on 14 June. He would return to the battalion and sadly be killed in action later at le Plessis Grimault. *(IWM B5529)*

Plaque on the church wall at Lingèvres to commemorate the men of 50th Infantry Division who fought here, and especially those who were killed. *(Author)*

During the afternoon of 15 June, elements of 231st Infantry Brigade also launched an attack on Hottot-les-Bagues, and eventually 1st Battalion, The Hampshire Regiment, forced its way in, only to be counter-attacked by tanks and ejected. Later, 2nd Battalion, The Devonshire Regiment, also fought its way into Hottot-les-Bagues, which it held all day despite several counter-attacks. The battalion was still there at last light but the brigade commander withdrew it, as the hold on the little town was so tenuous. The inevitable happened and Tilly-sur-Seulles was immediately re-occupied by the Germans. (Tilly was finally liberated on 17 June.)

After this failure 50th Infantry Division remained in close contact with the enemy but could make little progress. It was disposed with 69th Infantry Brigade on the right, south of Belle Épine and la Senaudière; 231st Infantry Brigade in the centre to the north of Hottot-les-Bagues; and 151st Infantry Brigade in the general area of Tilly-sur-Seulles.

For the rest of the month there would be little further forward movement in this sector. The DLI regimental history recounted how its various battalions inched their way down the road between Tilly-sur-Seulles and

Juvigny and had to fight for every field, hedgerow and building, with snipers and booby traps everywhere. It would be a long time before the 'Gateshead Gurkhas' forgot the *bocage*.

The scene at the regimental aid post of 9th DLI after the battle for Lingèvres, during which the battalion took heavy casualties including its commanding officer. (IWM B5527)

The Germans had turned Juvigny into a 'hedgehog' position, strongly defended with mortars and machine guns. The men of the Durham Light Infantry hit back with extensive daily patrolling, while the battalion snipers turned the tables on the enemy and caused them significant casualties. Then, on the night of 7/8 July, 70th Infantry Brigade (49th Infantry Division) took over and 151st Infantry Brigade went into divisional reserve for four days, just to the north of Lingèvres. The delights of clean clothes, baths, recreational visits to Bayeux, cinema and variety shows, plus the major boon of four untroubled nights' sleep quickly passed, then it was back into the line again, relieving 1st Battalion, The Dorsetshire Regiment, just north of Hottot-les-Bagues.

ON THE 'OTHER SIDE OF THE HILL'

Meanwhile life was just as difficult for the Panzer Lehr soldiers.

> *Major* (later *Oberst*) **Helmut Ritgen commented that they:**
>
> '... lived in the ground like foxes, under our panzers that were surrounded by earthen walls [to protect against shell fragments] ...We lived with danger both day and night. During the day, with a clear sky came the fighter-bombers, otherwise there was always artillery and mortar fire.'
>
> *Source:* Helmut Ritgen, *Memoirs of a Panzer Lehr Officer*, page 63.

Ritgen also explained how, if the Germans were able to counter-attack before the British were settled in (as at Hottot-les-Bagues), the Tommies could be pushed out of all their gains and the ground could be recaptured. However, this could not be done without sustaining losses, which were difficult to replace. Ritgen makes the point that, unlike the British who received replacements, the German units soon had noticeable gaps, especially in the officer corps, with the panzergrenadier units suffering the most.

CHAPTER 6

HEADS MUST ROLL

Despite the successes at Lingèvres and les Verrières, Hottot-les-Bagues was still in German hands and progress southwards was painfully slow. It was not until early July, and with 56th Infantry Brigade back under command again, that 50th Infantry Division was able to make any proper progress, the aim being to get across the main road to the west of Hottot-les-Bagues. This was finally achieved on 8 July, but not for long. The inevitable German counter-attack took place and forced the two leading battalions back north of the road again. And this was not the end of the German pressure. It was followed up at 0600 hours on 9 July by a three-company attack, supported by some 20–30 tanks. 2nd Essex was pushed back with heavy loss. Eight German tanks were knocked out, however.

Two days later, the three battalions of 231st Infantry Brigade, supported by the Nottinghamshire Yeomanry (Sherwood Rangers) endeavoured once again to take Hottot-les-Bagues. Their attack was preceded by a massive rolling artillery barrage, moving forward at the rate of 50 metres every two minutes, and with the length of the pauses on the various objectives being dictated by the infantry commanders taking part. Heavy fighting ensued, with severe casualties on both sides. By nightfall, the brigade had reached a line just north of Hottot-les-Bagues, but the Germans still held the village. A week later, on the night of 18/19 July, the Germans finally withdrew, not just from Hottot-les-Bagues, but also along the entire divisional front.

The 50th Division history refers to this event as the end of a phase of weeks of difficult fighting, which had yielded no great gains when measured in distance, but had 'slowly ground the enemy into impotence'. The Germans could no longer hold their line, but as always they withdrew 'not in rout, but carefully and steadily, with the usual array of booby traps and mines in [their] wake'. This belated success had only been achieved at a considerable price, the divisional losses by the end of June being 306 officers and 4,170 other ranks killed, wounded and missing.

Meanwhile 7th Armoured Division had also remained in roughly the same area as it had occupied after being withdrawn following the daring attack on Villers-Bocage. British troops would not enter the town again until 4 August when a patrol of 1st Dorsets went there, some two months behind schedule. 7th Armoured Division's history recounts this as being a nervy, anxious time, with just a steady drain of casualties to show for it all. There was no real task for the tanks, so the bulk of the hard work fell to the infantry. The infantry had to put up with holding a wide frontage day and night, with continual night patrols and little sleep even for those who did not go out on patrol (morning stand-to was 0415 hours and evening stand-to 2215 hours). Close liaison had been established with the neighbouring 1st US Infantry Division, with adjacent troops sharing emplacements, artillery and mortar support with the most amicable results. Then, at the end of June, the Desert Rats handed over their area to 2nd US Armored Division and were withdrawn back to a leaguer area north of Bucéels for, as their history puts it, 'a period of badly-needed rest and refitting'. In their brief three weeks in the *bocage* they had lost 1,149 all ranks.

'*Achtung Jabo!*' Two SS panzergrenadiers in Villers-Bocage keep a wary eye out for Allied fighter-bombers. (*Bundesarchiv 738/276/33a*)

These two divisions were of course just two of the 12 British divisions now ashore which, together with numerous independent brigades and a considerable 'tail', amounted to a fair-sized slice of the over one million Allied troops that had landed to that time. The German reserves facing them had been seriously depleted.

Two German infantry divisions had been cut off and destroyed in the Cherbourg peninsula and four others had been reduced to not much more than battle groups. In addition, the seven panzer divisions engaged had all suffered severely and still continued to do so under the never-ending air attacks which additionally made resupply and reinforcement so difficult. Some Germans calculated that it took as long to travel from eastern France to Normandy as it did from the depths of Poland to eastern France.

And to cap it all, the German High Command still anticipated an attack in the Pas de Calais area and thus kept divisions there, inactive and uncommitted to battle, which would have been extremely useful in Normandy. Looking back today it seems quite unbelievable that they did not smell a rat. Nevertheless, the Allies sensibly continued to maintain their deception plans, as it was in their best interests to do so for as long as possible, and the Germans went on believing them. In the circumstances, with only some 400,000 German soldiers committed to the battle, it is surprising that they were able to delay the Allied armies for so long. 'If we do not push inland shortly, we shall have to build skyscrapers to accommodate everyone!' was one of the jokes going around the beachhead. Some people even went as far as to predict that the battle for Normandy would degenerate into First World War-style trench warfare. One can therefore, readily imagine the frustration of the senior commanders during this period of stalemate.

The next major British offensive was code-named 'Epsom'. Like Perch, it sought to encircle Caen from the west. It was delayed by a terrible storm, so did not start properly until 26 June. That offensive and the other operations west of Caen are covered in detail in 'Battle Zone Normandy' *Operation Epsom*. Suffice it to say here that it was not until 10 July that most of Caen fell.

Eight days later, Second (British) Army would launch Operation 'Goodwood', the armoured assault south-east from Caen. All these important events, together with the US offensive Operation 'Cobra', are discussed in further volumes of the 'Battle Zone Normandy' series.

Here, however, it would be relevant to close by dealing with the direct results of Villers-Bocage as far as Second (British) Army was concerned in general, and the senior staff of XXX Corps, 7th Armoured Division and 22nd Armoured Brigade in particular.

Villers-Bocage under attack from RAF heavy bombers on 30 June. Some 266 aircraft dropped 4,000 tons of bombs from an altitude of 4,000 feet, virtually flattening the town. The raid was intended to block an attack by 2nd and 9th Panzer Divisions. Two bombers were lost. *(British Official)*

It was not until the first week of August that the changes actually took place. They were, however, 'on the cards' ever since Michael Wittmann decimated the Desert Rats' advance guard on 13 June.

General G.L. Verney, who took command of the division, explained the situation very tactfully:

'During the first week in August it was decided to make a number of changes in the Division. Numerous officers and men had fought for many months in the Desert, in Italy and in Normandy. It was General Montgomery's view that they should be given a spell in appointments or units where the vast experience they had gained could be turned to the training of the reinforcements who would shortly be coming overseas, or in posts where they would for a time be relieved of the strain of active service conditions in the front line.'

Source: G.L. Verney, *The Desert Rats*, page 215.

Lt-Gen Gerry Bucknall (*left*), commander of XXX Corps, seen here with his chief of staff, Brigadier Harold E. ('Pete') Pyman, a very competent ex-Royal Tank Regiment officer. Bucknall found it hard to adapt to fighting in the *bocage*, being too conventional and cautious. Monty would eventually replace him. (*IWM B5468*)

3rd CLY and 4th CLY met at Carpiquet airfield on 30 July, to amalgamate and become the 3rd/4th CLY under the command of Lt-Col W. Rankin (with cigarette). The unstoppable Captain Pat Dyas is also seen here, plus their crew. All wear the black rat of 4th Armoured Brigade with which they would serve for the rest of the war. *(National Army Museum)*

Despite these conciliatory remarks, which were echoed in the official history of the campaign when it was published, Verney was initially quite scornful about his new command, saying (in August 1944) that when they came back from Italy they were 'extremely swollen-headed... and a law unto themselves: they thought they need only obey those orders that suited them.' He then commented on their bad march discipline and ended by saying that they 'greatly deserved the criticism they received'.

Montgomery was equally annoyed and critical of those he considered responsible, writing in a letter to a friend:

'I have had to get rid of a few people you know. Bucknall could not manage a Corps once the battle became mobile and I have Jorrocks [Lt-Gen Horrocks] in his place in 30 Corps. Bullen-Smith could do nothing with 51 Div so had to go. Thomas Rennie is there now and the Division is quite different under him. 7th Armd Div went right down and failed badly so I removed Bobbie [Erskine] who had become very sticky and put in Verney of the Gds Tank brigade. I also had to remove Loony Hinde; I have put Mackeson to 22nd Armoured Brigade.'

Source: Nigel Hamilton, *Monty: Master of the Battlefield*, pp. 804–5.

General Sir Brian Horrocks suggested some reasons for the veterans' difficulties in Normandy, commenting in his autobiography:

'Another disturbing feature was the comparative lack of success of the veteran 7th Armoured and 51st Highland Divisions. Both came again later on and finished the war in magnificent shape, but during the Normandy fighting they were not at their best... after being lionised in the UK, [they] came out to Normandy and found themselves faced with an entirely different type of battle, fought under different conditions of terrain. And they began to see the differences all too clearly. A racing enthusiast once described the condition to me as being "like an old plater who won't go in the mud". All the more credit to them that they eventually staged a come-back and regained their Middle East form.'

Source: B.G. Horrocks, *A Full Life*.

To be fair to the Desert Rats and to those whom Monty sacked I believe the remarks made at the start of Chapter 1 apply very strongly, especially concerning their main equipment, particularly the Cromwell tank. In the close *bocage* fighting it was invariably on a hiding to nothing due to its vulnerability and lack of firepower. The Cromwell's effectiveness undoubtedly improved when the close country was left behind and good mobility became more important. However, that still did not improve its

This knocked-out Cromwell in Villers-Bocage was the tank of 4th CLY's Regimental Sergeant-Major Gerald Holloway. He almost managed to reverse to the bend behind him, and must have cursed the fact that the Cromwell was painfully slow in reverse gear. *(Bundesarchiv 101/494/3376/19a)*

firepower or its protection, the other two primary characteristics of a tank.

Why the British Army should have continually expected its brave tank crews to have risked their all in inferior tanks is beyond belief. Yet this was not the first time this had happened. It was only when the Comet tank was in service from after the Rhine crossing in 1945 that British forces had a medium tank which began to compare with the Panther and Tiger, which had by then been in operational service for two or more years.

I leave the last words on this subject to an infantryman, a 'Gateshead Gurkha'.

Major Roy Griffiths wrote after the war:

'Some books I read after the war about morale of the troops who came back from the desert, that the reason why there was a slow advance in Normandy was because we were rather wary of and inexperienced in the Bocage country because we were so used to the wide open spaces

The Bayeux War Cemetery is the largest Commonwealth war cemetery in France and the most cosmopolitan, with 4,649 graves, British, Australian, Canadian, New Zealand, South African, Polish, French, Czech, Italian, Russian and German; 4,219 of the dead have been identified. It is on the western side of the ring road opposite the Musée Memorial 1944 Bataille de Normandie. *(Author)*

of the desert. But no-one was experienced in the Bocage country.

There were these high hedges at the sides of the roads and no-one was experienced and the people who got the most stick, quite honestly, were the lads in the tanks, because they couldn't see. They could see straight up the roads but they couldn't see over the high hedges and what was in the cornfields... It is true to say, that when we achieved our objectives we were never pushed off. What we took we held always and to say that morale was low in 50th Infantry Division or 7th Armd Div is absolute arrant nonsense and it makes my blood boil.'

Source: Quoted in Harry Moses, *The Gateshead Gurkhas.*

Major Griffiths blames the *bocage* countryside and I am much of his opinion. And we are in good company because the Supreme Allied Commander, General Dwight D. Eisenhower, himself came to an identical conclusion. As he explained in his book *Crusade in Europe*, on one occasion when he was feeling

particularly frustrated by the seeming lack of progress being made on the ground despite great efforts he determined to see for himself just what was causing all the hold-ups in the battle area.

'One day a few of us visited a forward observation tower located on a hill, which took us to a height of about a hundred feet above the surrounding hedgerows. Our vision was [still] so limited that I called upon the air forces to take me in a fighter plane along the battlefront in an effort to gain a clear impression of what we were up against. Unfortunately, even from the vantage point of an altitude of several thousand feet, there was not much to see that could be classed as helpful.'

The 49th Infantry Division memorial opposite Fontenay-le-Pesnel Cemetery. (Author)

HISTORY

Eisenhower goes on to say that under such conditions he considered that it had to be what he described as 'dogged "doughboy" fighting at its worst'.

Rightly, therefore one must come to the inescapable conclusion that a brave, resolute and well equipped defender could undoubtedly gain many advantages from the terrain in Normandy, especially when the attacker was continually bogged down by the suffocating grip of the all-entangling *bocage*. Of course it is only right to point out that, if and when the attacker could secure a firm foothold, then it was virtually impossible for the defender to eject him also, but that did really not make progress any faster. Thus, for both sides, the only way through such a maze was by shedding blood, sweat and tears – and they were shed in abundance in the *bocage* in the summer of 1944.

Bloody but unbowed. After five days of almost continuous fighting, this 4th CLY crew is at last able to cook a meal and perhaps get some sleep. *(IWM B5681)*

PART THREE

BATTLEFIELD TOURS

GENERAL TOURING INFORMATION

Normandy is a thriving holiday area, with some beautiful countryside, excellent beaches and very attractive architecture (particularly in the case of religious buildings). It was also, of course, the scene of heavy fighting in 1944, and this has had a considerable impact on the tourist industry. To make the most of your trip, especially if you intend visiting non-battlefield sites, we strongly recommend you purchase one of the general Normandy guidebooks that are commonly available. These include: *Michelin Green Guide: Normandy*; *Thomas Cook Travellers: Normandy*; *The Rough Guide to Brittany and Normandy*; *Lonely Planet: Normandy*.

TRAVEL REQUIREMENTS

First, make sure you have the proper documentation to enter France as a tourist. Citizens of European Union countries, including Great Britain, should not usually require visas, but will need to carry and show their passports. Others should check with the French Embassy in their own country before travelling. British citizens should also fill in and take Form E111 (available from main post offices), which deals with entitlement to medical treatment, and all should consider taking out comprehensive travel insurance. France is part of the Eurozone, and you should also check exchange rates before travelling.

GETTING THERE

The most direct routes from the UK to Lower Normandy are by ferry from Portsmouth to Ouistreham (near Caen), and from Portsmouth or Poole to Cherbourg. Depending on which you choose, and whether you travel by day or night, the crossing takes between four and seven hours. Alternatively, you can sail to Le Havre, Boulogne or Calais and drive the rest of the way. (Travel time from Calais to Caen is about four hours; motorway

Above: The ancient town of Bayeux and its environs form an ideal base for this tour. It is full of a wealth of architectural heritage like the cathedral and also has the famous Bayeux Tapestry. *(Author)*

Page 111: A *Schwimmwagen* amphibious light car halted in the small square near the bandstand in Villers-Bocage. Note the Tiger in the background, which is near the town hall. *(Bundesarchiv 101/738/276/34a)*

and bridge tolls may be payable depending on the exact route taken.) Another option is to use the Channel Tunnel. Whichever way you decide to travel, early booking is advised, especially during the summer months.

Although you can of course hire motor vehicles in Normandy, the majority of visitors from the UK or other EU countries will probably take their own. If you do so, you will also need to take: a full driving licence; your vehicle registration document; a certificate of motor insurance valid in France (your insurer will advise on this); spare headlight and indicator bulbs; headlight beam adjusters or tape; a warning triangle; and a sticker or number plate identifying which country the vehicle is registered in. Visitors from elsewhere should consult a motoring organisation in their home country for details of the documents and other items they will require.

Normandy's road system is well developed, although there are still a few choke points, especially around the larger towns during rush hour and in the holiday season. As a general guide, in clear conditions it is possible to drive from Cherbourg to Caen in less than two hours.

Special recommendations

The author stayed on the outskirts of Bayeux at the *Ferme-Manoir au Pont Rouge*, St-Loup Hors (tel: 33 (0)2 31 22 39 09). It is run by an English couple, Michael and Rosemary Chilcott, and is a highly recommended B&B.

There are many places to eat in Bayeux, some being listed in the tourist office leaflet. Two which are not listed, but which are well worth a visit, are: *le Petit Normand*, 35 Rue Larcher, near the cathedral; and *la Rapière*, 53 Rue Saint Jean. Both serve excellent food at reasonable prices.

There are plenty of good places to stay – here, for example, is the Ferme-Manoir au Pont Rouge at St-Loup Hors, near Bayeux. *(Author)*

ACCOMMODATION

Accommodation in Normandy is plentiful and diverse, from cheap campsites to five star hotels in glorious châteaux. However, early booking is advised if you wish to travel between June and August. The obvious place to stay for those interested in the Villers-Bocage battles is Bayeux. Details of accommodation in and around the town are contained in a free leaflet (in English) entitled: 'Bayeux and the Region' available from Bayeux tourist office (*listed below*). The leaflet also has a street map of Bayeux, details of attractions and so on. Alternatively, you can base yourself slightly further afield; the historic city of Caen, for example, has over 60 hotels. Useful contacts include:

French Travel Centre, 178 Piccadilly, London W1V 0AL;
   tel: 0870 830 2000; web: www.raileurope.co.uk
French Tourist Authority, 444 Madison Avenue, New York,
   NY 10022 (other offices in Chicago, Los Angeles and Miami);
   web: www.francetourism.com
Office de Tourisme Intercommunal de Bayeux, Pont Saint-Jean,
   14400 Bayeux; tel: +33 (0)2 31 51 28 28;
   web: www.bayeux-tourism.com
Office de Tourisme du Pre-Bocage, Place Charles de Gaulle,
   14310 Villers-Bocage; tel: +33 (0)2 31 77 16 14;
   email: otpb@tiscali.fr
Calvados Tourisme, Place du Canada, 14000 Caen;
   tel: +33 (0)2 31 86 53 30; web: www.calvados-tourisme.com
Manche Tourisme; web: www.manchetourisme.com
Maison du Tourisme de Cherbourg et du Haut-Cotentin,
   2 Quai Alexandre III, 50100 Cherbourg-Octeville;
   tel: +33 (0)2 33 93 52 02; web: www.ot-cherbourg-cotentin.fr
Gîtes de France, La Maison des Gîtes de France et du Tourisme
   Vert, 59 Rue Saint-Lazare, 75 439 Paris Cedex 09;
   tel: +33 (0)1 49 70 75 75; web: www.gites-de-france.fr

BATTLEFIELD TOURING

Each volume in the 'Battle Zone Normandy' series contains three or more battlefield tours. These are intended to last from a few hours to a full day apiece. Some are best undertaken using motor transport, others should be done on foot, and many involve a mixture of the two. Owing to its excellent infrastructure and relatively gentle topography, Normandy also makes a good location for a cycling holiday; indeed, some of our tours are ideally suited to this method.

In every case the tour author has visited the area concerned recently, so the information presented should be accurate and reasonably up to date. Nevertheless land use, infrastructure and rights of way can change, sometimes at short notice. If you encounter difficulties in following any tour, we would very much like to hear about it, so we can incorporate changes in future editions. Your comments should be sent to the publisher at the address provided at the front of this book.

To derive maximum value and enjoyment from the tours, we suggest you equip yourself with the following items:

- Appropriate maps. European road atlases can be purchased from a wide range of locations outside France. However, for navigation within Normandy, the French Institut Géographique National (IGN) produces maps at a variety of scales (www.ign.fr). The 1:100,000 series ('Top 100') is particularly useful when driving over larger distances; sheet 06 (Caen – Cherbourg) covers most of the invasion area. For pinpointing locations precisely, the current IGN 1:25,000 Série Bleue is best (extracts from this series are used for the tour maps in this book). These can be purchased in many places across Normandy. They can also be ordered in the UK from some bookshops, or from specialist dealers such as the Hereford Map Centre, 24–25 Church Street, Hereford HR1 2LR; tel: 01432 266322; web: <www.themapcentre.com>. Allow at least a fortnight's notice, although some maps may be in stock. The Série Bleue sheets required to cover the areas discussed in this book are: 1512OT Bayeux, 1413E Caumont-l'Éventé and 1513O Aunay-sur-Odon/Villers-Bocage.
- Lightweight waterproof clothing and robust footwear are essential, especially for touring in the countryside.
- Take a compass, provided you know how to use one!
- A camera and spare films/memory cards.
- A notebook to record what you have photographed.
- A French dictionary and/or phrasebook. (English is widely spoken in the coastal area, but is much less common inland.)
- Food and drink. Although you are never very far in Normandy from a shop, restaurant or *tabac*, many of the tours do not pass directly by such facilities. It is therefore sensible to take some light refreshment with you.
- Binoculars. Most officers and some other ranks carried binoculars in 1944. Taking a pair adds a surprising amount of verisimilitude to the touring experience.

SOME DO'S AND DON'TS

Battlefield touring can be an extremely interesting and even emotional experience, especially if you have read something about the battles beforehand. In addition, it is fair to say that residents of Normandy are used to visitors, among them battlefield tourers, and generally will do their best to help if you encounter problems. However, many of the tours in the 'Battle Zone Normandy' series are off the beaten track, and you can expect some puzzled looks from the locals, especially inland. In all cases we have tried to ensure that tours are on public land, or viewable from public rights of way. However, in the unlikely event that you are asked to leave a site, do so immediately and by the most direct route.

Not far to the south of the battlefield area is the beautiful countryside of la Suisse Normande, which also has many hotels and inns. (Author)

In addition: **Never remove 'souvenirs' from the battlefields.** Even today it is not unknown for farmers to turn up relics of the 1944 fighting. Taking these without permission may not only be illegal, but can be extremely dangerous. It also ruins the site for genuine battlefield archaeologists. Anyone returning from France should also remember customs regulations on the import of weapons and ammunition of any kind.

Be especially careful when investigating fortifications. Some of the more frequently-visited sites are well preserved, and several of them have excellent museums. However, both along the coast and inland there are numerous positions that have been left to decay, and which carry risks for the unwary. In particular, remember that many of these places were the scenes of heavy fighting or subsequent demolitions, which may have caused severe (and sometimes invisible) structural damage. Coastal erosion has also undermined the foundations of a number of shoreline defences. Under no circumstances should underground bunkers, chambers and tunnels be entered, and care should always be taken when examining above-ground structures. If in any doubt, stay away.

Beware of hunting (shooting) areas (signposted *Chasse Gardée*). Do not enter these, even if they offer a short cut to your destination. Similarly, Normandy contains a number of restricted areas (military facilities and wildlife reserves), which should be avoided. Watch out, too, for temporary footpath closures, especially along sections of coastal cliffs.

If using a motor vehicle, keep your eyes on the road. There are many places to park, even on minor routes, and it is always better to turn round and retrace your path than to cause an accident. In rural areas avoid blocking entrances and driving along farm tracks; again, it is better to walk a few hundred metres than to cause damage and offence.

GENERAL MILITARY TOURING

As far as D-Day and the Battle of Normandy as a whole are concerned an excellent leaflet, again in English, is available from all tourist offices, entitled 'The D-Day Landings and the Battle of Normandy', which lists all the relevant museums in the area.

The most important museum as far as the battles of the *bocage* are concerned is the *Bayeux Memorial Museum*, which is located on the Bayeux ring road at Boulevard Fabian Ware. If you only visit one museum in Normandy then make sure this is the one. Its spectacular, relevant collection, its excellent displays and good interpretation, raise it head and shoulders above all the rest. In Sector IV of the museum, for example, there is much that is relevant to the battles around Tilly-sur-Seulles and Villers-Bocage.

Bayeux Memorial Museum

Musée Mémorial de la Bataille de Normandie,
Boulevard Fabian Ware, 14400 Bayeux; tel: +33 (0)2 31 51 46 90; email: <museedelabataille@free.fr>. Open 0930–1830 daily 1 May–15 Sept, otherwise 1000–1200 & 1400–1800 daily, closed for 2 weeks in Jan. Entrance fee.

Outside the museum are various small monuments, for example to the men of The Essex Regiment and those of the Nottinghamshire Yeomanry (Sherwood Rangers). Very close to

Poor Villers-Bocage was bombed almost flat by the Allies as this photograph shows. This view was taken looking to the south-east. *(IWM CL913)*

And it looked just as bad at ground level! Here, two French policemen chat with a British officer on Place Richard Lenoir. Note the 'TT' symbol (Tees & Tyne) of the 50th Infantry Division on the base of a destroyed statue. *(IWM B8639)*

this excellent museum is the *Bayeux Memorial*, which stands opposite the war cemetery and bears the names (1,808 in all) of men of the Commonwealth forces who died in the Battle of Normandy and have no known grave. The *Bayeux War Cemetery* (4,144 Commonwealth burials) is the largest Second World War Commonwealth cemetery in France. It contains burials of men brought in from the surrounding districts and from hospitals that were located nearby. If you have connections to the Rifle Brigade, then it is also worthwhile visiting the small church of St-Exupère, just off the Eisenhower roundabout on the ring road, where five members of 1st Rifle Brigade are buried.

NON-MILITARY SITES

Bayeux contains a host of other sites of interest, such as the world-famous Bayeux Tapestry, the Cathédrale Nôtre-Dame and the Hôtel du Doyen, all of which are well worth visiting. Also nearby is the district known as la Suisse Normande, an area of outstanding natural beauty south of Thury-Harcourt along the valley of the River Orne, easily within striking distance of Bayeux or Caen; a fascinating extension to the *bocage* and certainly pleasant to tour.

YOUR IMAGINATION

In addition to the equipment already listed, one of the things which it is vital that you take in abundance is your imagination. In 1944 much of the countryside to the south of Bayeux was dominated by the *bocage* – a close meshed network of small fields, thick hedgerows, pollarded trees and sunken roads – aptly described as 'the Cotswold country superimposed on Salisbury Plain'. It has now been altered out of all recognition, many of the hedgerows having been grubbed up to make it easier to use modern farm machinery. Examples of the real *bocage* can still be found, however (*see opposite*). A visit to such an area will help to get the 'feel' of how limited was the field of vision and how difficult it must have been to maintain contact and surveillance. Whilst obscuring the view, the hedgerows provided little protection from fire, indirect artillery and mortar rounds with sensitive fuses, for example, being detonated on trees and bushes. Undoubtedly it meant that the defender generally had an advantage over the attacker.

In addition, new metalled roads, new farm buildings and many

The Bocage

The photograph shows a typical *bocage* lane/sunken road, which is how many roads/tracks must have appeared in June 1944. This example, one of a number near Bayeux, is in between the villages of Brunville, Ranchy and Subles, about 3 km to the south-west of the town.

Look around the minor roads and tracks in this area, for example the unmade road over the River Drôme that crosses two small stone bridges beside le Moulin (the mill). Leave your car at the road/track junction and walk down to the river. DO NOT attempt to drive down to the stream, as the track is narrow and twisty and the two bridges are far too narrow! However, it will give you a good impression of what much of the *bocage* must have been like in June 1944. There are other similar examples in the same area, including some on the road marked *Tour du Bessin* on the map. In this way you will be able to fix firmly in your mind what the *bocage* countryside of 1944 was really like before embarking on any of the tours.

The lane to Ranchy over the River Drôme gives a good idea of the state of many roads and tracks in the *bocage* in 1944, before the countryside was opened up by modern farming methods. Look also at the wartime aerial photographs, showing the much tighter field pattern. *(Author)*

other new dwellings have changed the face of the countryside completely. Whole villages, and even small towns such as Villers-Bocage, were also completely flattened by bombing, so that very little of the old remains. Fortunately Bayeux itself is an exception and has many old buildings and interesting places to visit, both connected and unconnected with this study. However, this means that modern maps, which are essential to getting around now, are very different to those used in wartime. Nowhere is this more obvious than at Villers-Bocage, where a new road (the N175) has been built alongside the old D675, which itself was built alongside an even older road/track, making it slightly tricky to find exact locations. The all-important Point 213 is now called Point 217 on the new map just to add to the fun!

THE VILLERS-BOCAGE TOURS

The tours that follow have a common theme, namely the impact that a brave, well-trained tank commander can have on a battle. Tour A begins with coverage of the approach march to Villers-Bocage but if time is short then the advance phase could be taken as read and the tour started at Point 213, having driven to Villers-Bocage directly down the N175.

All of the tours are suitable for cyclists, as is most of the surrounding area. The only really hilly part is the Suisse Normande district to the south, but the views are well worth the effort. Access for those with mobility difficulties should not generally be a problem. Most sites are either accessible to wheelchairs or at least viewable from a nearby metalled road. The only building that might prove tricky is the Battle of Tilly-sur-Seulles Museum in its little chapel which is down a bank, although there is a well-surfaced path.

Specialist Help in Villers-Bocage

If you have time (and it is open), then it is a good idea to visit the town hall in Place de Maréchal Leclerc, as there is a detailed model of what Villers-Bocage looked like prior to the battle. In addition, one of the real experts on the battle lives in Villers-Bocage, namely M. Henri Marie, a local historian and author. He is prepared to assist visitors to the town BUT ideally by prior arrangement! You can contact him at: 29 Boulevard du 13 Juin 1944, 14310 Villers-Bocage, if possible, before you visit. Other places through which he is contactable are the town hall, the tourist office (*details on p. 115*) and his son's pharmacy at 23 Rue Georges Clemenceau.

TOUR A

VILLERS-BOCAGE: FIRST BATTLE, 12–13 JUNE

OBJECTIVE: A tour following the advance by 7th Armoured Division from its leaguer area through Villers-Bocage to Point 213 and then covering Wittmann's devastating counter-attack.

DURATION: The route from St-Paul-du-Vernay to Villers-Bocage is approximately 25 km.

St-Paul-du-Vernay, 3 km west-southwest of the leaguer area at Trungy. This was the starting point for the right flanking advance of 7th Armoured Division to Villers-Bocage. *(Author)*

APPROACH TO BATTLE: As explained in the history section, 7th Armoured Division launched a daring 'right hook' deep into German-held territory to take the high ground at Point 213 to the north-east of Villers-Bocage. The advance was led by a 4th County of London Yeomanry (CLY) group (Lt-Col Viscount Cranley) and began at 1600 hours on 12 June 1944 from the division's leaguer in the Trungy area. Operating in front and to

To LA BUTTE and
ST-PAUL-DU-VERNAY

VILLERS-BOCA

Base maps: IGN 1413E, IGN 1512OT, IGN 1513O

the flanks of the 4th CLY group, which was the division's advance guard, were two reconnaissance units – 8th Hussars (7th Armoured Division's reconnaissance regiment) and 11th Hussars (XXX Corps' reconnaissance regiment). A Company, 1st Rifle Brigade, (Major J. Wright) was in direct support of 4th CLY and was travelling behind A Squadron (Major P. Scott), the leading squadron. In addition, two OP tanks belonging to 5th RHA were up with the advance guard. (*See page 51 for order of march.*) One of the tank commanders told the author that most of the roads used were tarmac, but edged with *bocage* hedgerows.

Stand A1: Livry

DIRECTIONS: The tour starts at the village of St-Paul-du-Vernay, through which 7th Armoured Division's leading elements passed soon after leaving the Trungy area on the afternoon of 12 June. To reach St-Paul-du-Vernay from Bayeux, the most straightforward route is via the D6, which runs south-east in an almost straight line for 12 km to Tilly-sur-Seulles. Following this route also gives some sense of the distances involved in 7th Armoured Division's abortive first attempt to push south towards

These substantial houses in the centre of Briquessard village were probably there during wartime. The village, however, like so many others in the area, now looks far more prosperous and well cared for. (*Author*)

Villers-Bocage. At the crossroads in the centre of Tilly-sur-Seulles turn right (west) onto the D13 and follow the road through Lingèvres, la Senaudière and Belle Épine for about 10 km until you reach the crossroads at the southern end of St-Paul-du-Vernay (marked as la Butte on the IGN map 1512OT). Here, turn left onto the D99, very close to the start of the route marked on the map on page 124. From here follow the D99 southwards through Cahagnolles and Ste-Honorine-de-Ducy, then on towards St-Martin le Vieux. At St-Martin take the left hand fork, the D115, for 1.5 km into Livry, crossing the D9 just before you enter the village. Pause at Livry, pulling to the side of the road where it is safe to do so.

THE ACTION: The head of the column reached the Livry area at about 1900 hours, where it made its first contact. There were some infantry in the village and an anti-tank gun which knocked out one of the leading 8th Hussars Cromwells. One 1st Rifle Brigade platoon was then detailed to deal with the German position, which was cleared by about 2000 hours. Brigadier Hinde then decided that to move on any further in the dark would not only be foolish but, as they would soon be turning east towards Amayé-sur-Seulles, it could give away their objective (Villers-Bocage) to the Germans. The column therefore halted approximately on the line of the modern D9 road. However, reconnaissance still continued to probe, looking for the shoulder of the German positions (Panzer Lehr Division) around which the column would have to pass. A troop of 8th Hussars made contact some 3 km to the east and lost its two leading Cromwells in the fire-fight that followed.

Pause on leaving Livry and just think about what sort of a night the advance guard must have spent out in the middle of German territory. Vehicles had to be replenished, crews fed and so on, while for the officers, tank and section commanders there were always the inevitable orders groups to attend, maps to mark up and information to pass on to sections and crews, so little sleep was possible. Add to this the fact that it rained during the night, so everyone got up wet. The advance began again at about 0530 hours and the weather improved slightly as the sunshine broke through. Now deep within enemy territory, progress would have been slow and deliberate, tank troops advancing using standardised advance-to-contact drills, so that the leading tank

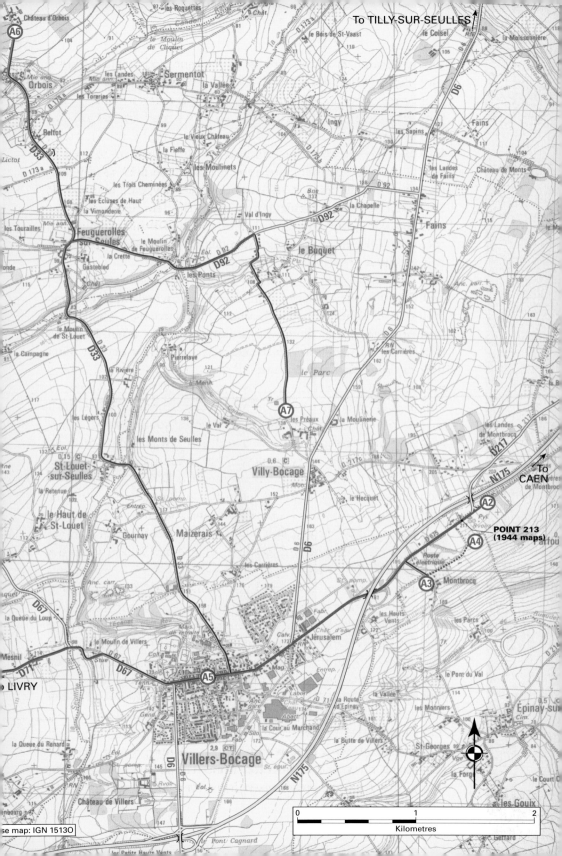

To TILLY-SUR-SEULLES

To CAEN

POINT 213
(1944 maps)

Villers-Bocage

To LIVRY

Château d'Orbois
Orbois
Sermentot
Feuguerolles-sur-Seulles
le Buquet
Fains
Château de Monts
Villy-Bocage
St-Louet-sur-Seulles
le Haut de St-Louet
Maizerais
Montbrocq
Épinay-sur-
Château de Villers

Base map: IGN 1513O

0   1   2
Kilometres

was always covered forward by at least one other tank from a static fire position or corner.

Stand A2: Point 213

DIRECTIONS: Continue on the D115 through Livry and on to Briquessard. At Briquessard join the D71 heading south-east. Continue on the D71 past Amayé-sur-Seulles until it joins the D67 after le Mesnil, some 7 km in all from Briquessard. Pause here to take in the view of Villers-Bocage and then continue into the town. Of course the little town has grown considerably since it was rebuilt after the war. Compare the pre-war photographs of the road into and through Villers-Bocage (*opposite and pages 65 and 73*) with the modern scene. Drive slowly up along the main street (Rue Pasteur – Rue Georges Clemenceau) towards the north-eastern end of the town, in the direction of Point 213. The tour will return to the centre but it is worth just getting one's bearings generally at this stage.

Le Mesnil, the last hamlet on the the D71 before Villers-Bocage. *(Author)*

Leave the town centre and pass the D6 turning on the left, continuing through the suburb of Jérusalem and on towards the new N175 road. However, make sure that you stay on the old

Entry to Villers-Bocage, showing the current environs to the west on the D71/D67. Compare this with the pre-war view below and the aerial and other photos earlier in the book. *(Author)*

Villers-Bocage. This is a pre-war photograph of the western end of town leading into Place Jeanne d'Arc via Rue Pasteur. To the left is the road to Caumont-l'Éventé, to the right the road to Vire. *(Henri Marie)*

Looking south-west back towards Villers Bocage from the *poste électrique* on the D675. The turning to Montbrocq is just visible on the same side as the *poste*. Wittmann drove along this lane from the south to join the D675 from his overnight position in the broken ground just north of Montbrocq. Almost immediately he began engaging the western end of the A Squadron column, effectively isolating the A Squadron tanks from the rest of the force. *(Author)*

Reservoirs at Point 213 on the south side of the D675. It was in this field that the leading tanks of A Squadron, 4th CLY, started to take up positions, not suspecting that there were already German tanks to their south-west. *(Author)*

D675 road and NOT the new highway, which should be on your left as you near the top of the hill. Go on past an electricity station on the right hand side, then a small track junction on the left-hand side next to a house. Stop in the lay-by just beside some reservoirs in the field to your right. You are now almost at Point 213, which was just where the D217 road leaves the D675 to cross the N175 *en route* for Villy-Bocage. The field with the reservoirs and the one to its south are where part of A Squadron, 4th CLY deployed. The reservoirs are marked on the IGN map by the modern spot height of 217 metres.

THE ACTION: The head of the 4th CLY and A Company,

1st Rifle Brigade, advance guard had reached Villers-Bocage at about 0830 hours. They were given a warm welcome by those citizens who had stayed behind despite the artillery fire which had been landing in the streets for some days, and it took about half an hour for the head of the column to reach Point 213, where it halted. Major Wright had decided to hold an orders group at Point 213 for his platoon commanders, so they were being picked up in three half-tracks and brought up to the head of the column. Meanwhile, A Squadron, 4th CLY's leading tanks were getting off the road and into the fields alongside to the south. Tank crews, like the infantry, were all fairly relaxed and some had even started to brew up. Lt-Col Lord Cranley, however, did not share this mood of relaxation as he was far too worried that they were 'out on a limb'.

Brigadier Hinde, who was 'swanning' in his scout car, came up to talk to Cranley to reassure him that all would be well. Hinde told Cranley to go forward to Point 213 and see A Squadron's Major Scott to check that he was in a good defensive position. Cranley reached Point 213 safely before Wittmann began his assault on the column, but of course this meant that he was taken prisoner later. Brigadier Hinde must have then gone back to his tactical headquarters at Amayé-sur-Seulles and took no further active part in the first battle.

Before going any further, it would be sensible to fix in your mind exactly where all the vehicles in the column were located. As will be seen regimental headquarters was well up behind the leading squadron/company group, whilst B Squadron and the rest of the regimental column were only just entering the town. Circumstances, mainly the need to pass on orders, had unfortunately led to a concentration of some senior commanders at the head of the column and had thus isolated them from their troops when the action began.

This broken ground between the *poste électrique* and Montbrocq is the probable location of Wittmann's overnight leaguer position. *(Author)*

While everything was deceptively quiet at Point 213 and down the road to Villers-Bocage, 4th CLY Group was in fact in terrible danger. Unbeknown to them, German tanks were already ensconced on the Point 213 feature. They were part of 2nd Company, 101st Heavy SS Panzer Battalion, under the command of the redoubtable SS-Lieutenant Michael Wittmann. They had been driving for some days all the way from the Belgian border, via Paris, and had been subjected to repeated attacks from fighter-bombers. In addition, the notoriously weak transmissions of their Tiger tanks had not been helped by having to travel such a long distance along poor roads. Some of the Tigers had broken down and so there were only six of the original company remaining when they reached Point 213, at least two of which were having problems with either engine or transmission. One of the breakdowns *en route* had been Wittmann's own tank, so the six that arrived were (commanders' names in brackets): No. 211 (Wessel), No. 221 (Hantusch), No. 222 (Sowa), No. 223 (Brendt), No. 233 (Lötzsch) and No. 234 (Stief). Wessel had gone off to make contact with Panzer Lehr Division, whilst Stief's Tiger was overheating and Lötzsch's had a damaged track, so only three were fully fit. A second company of ten Tigers, under SS-Captain Rolf Möbius, which had been following Wittmann's company down the D675, had leaguered about 16 km away to the east.

Stand A3: Montbrocq

DIRECTIONS: Wittmann had positioned his Tigers in a leaguer area near Montbrocq (la Cidrerie). To get there, go back about 700 metres along the D675 towards Villers-Bocage and turn left just past the electricity station. Stop near the Montbrocq crossroads after 200 metres.

THE ACTION: The Tigers were positioned, well camouflaged, in the broken ground near Montbrocq. They had spent the night there being troubled by sporadic artillery fire, but had seen no British troops. One can well imagine the surprise, therefore, of the *Waffen-SS* crews when they first heard, then saw as it got closer, the British column coming out of Villers-Bocage and then halting at Point 213, just a few hundred metres away from them.

Wittmann got into the nearest Tiger (Stief's) and ordered its

Michael Wittmann

SS-Obersturmführer Michael Wittmann was already an acknowledged German tank ace, with a formidable tally of tanks and anti-tank guns to his credit – over 100 of each – which he had knocked out in actions on the Russian Front. A 30-year-old Bavarian, he had been commanding an armoured car when the war began and was still under training when the German *Blitzkrieg* swept through France in the summer of 1940. His first campaign was in the Balkans, but it was the invasion of Russia, from June 1941, that saw him rise to prominence. By then, as a member of the *Waffen-SS*, he was commanding a *Sturmgeschütz* (self-propelled assault gun) and was awarded the Iron Cross 2nd Class, then 1st Class, that summer. In the spring of 1943, he joined the *Leibstandarte* Division's 13th SS Panzer Regiment. The unit was equipped with the new Tiger tank and by 1944 Wittmann was a renowned 'Tiger ace' with the Knight's Cross with Oakleaves as visible proof of his bravery. And by now he was becoming increasingly well-known in Germany, his undoubted skill and courage being cleverly manipulated by the German propaganda machine, so that he had become a household name even before Villers-Bocage. For his bravery at Villers-Bocage he would be promoted to *SS-Hauptsturmführer* (Captain) and awarded the coveted Swords to his Knight's Cross. He was killed on 8 August, when his Tiger was knocked out by Sherman Fireflies of the Northamptonshire Yeomanry at Gaumesnil, south of Caen (see 'Battle Zone Normandy' *Road to Falaise*).

Photo: Bundesarchiv 299/1802/8

commander to advance. However, it was soon very clear that it was having engine trouble, so he got out and climbed into No. 222, leaving its commander (Sowa) to explain to the others what was happening. As he moved off down the track towards the main road, he was spotted by one of the 1st Rifle Brigade NCOs (Sergeant O'Connor of 1st Platoon) who was on his way up to the orders group, and who came on the air with a frantic warning.

Montbrocq hamlet from the track past the *poste électrique* where it meets the old track into Villers-Bocage that runs roughly parallel with the D675. *(Author)*

It was now about 0900 hours and the German tank opened fire – initially engaging an A Squadron Cromwell (still on the road), followed by a Sherman Firefly behind it that was in the act of traversing onto the Tiger. Both burst into flames and the Firefly slewed across the road, blocking it to any withdrawal back to Villers-Bocage or reinforcement of Point 213, where the other A Squadron Cromwells were now being engaged by two of Wittmann's Tigers.

Stand A4: Wittmann's Rampage

DIRECTIONS: Walk down the lane running to the north-east from the Montbrocq crossroads (parallel with the D675) past the very obvious broken ground on your left and the new houses to your right. This lane comes out by the field in which the

The knocked-out Cromwell of Lieutenant John Cloudsley-Thompson, troop leader of RHQ Troop, 4th CLY. After his tank was knocked out, he and his crew baled out unhurt, despite heavy machine-gun fire all around them. After hiding in various places until dark, they then wandered about the battlefield, at times very close to German positions. Fortunately they eventually managed to reach British lines and were safely evacuated. *(Bundesarchiv 1494/3376/20a)*

reservoirs are now located and is most probably the way the Tigers approached their enemy. Return to the crossroads, go back to the D675 and turn left downhill towards Villers-Bocage. As you do so, imagine that you are Wittmann in his Tiger as he motored down the road, destroying the half-tracks of A Company and the carriers of the anti-tank section as he went. As he passed the road junction on the edge of town (D6 Tilly-sur-Seulles road) he would have come level with the three Stuart light tanks of Reconnaissance Troop, 4th CLY, which proved no hindrance to the massive Tiger as it lumbered on into town.

THE ACTION: Now it was the turn of 4th CLY's RHQ Troop to face the onslaught. First, just a few metres behind the Stuarts, were the four RHQ Troop tanks (second-in-command, RHQ troop leader, adjutant – shared by the commanding officer when mounted – and regimental sergeant-major). They were followed by the two 5th RHA OP tanks (one Sherman OP with wooden gun and one Cromwell OP). Realising that there was deadly danger ahead, they all desperately began to try to reverse and to look for cover. However, the Cromwell was noted for being very slow in reverse, so all found it hard to escape – all that is apart from Captain Pat Dyas, who managed to back off into a small garden of a house on the southern side of the road. The Tiger passed close by him did not spot him. Dyas would have loved to have got a side shot at the Tiger as it passed, but unfortunately he was without his gunner, who had earlier got out of the tank to relieve himself and vanished. So, while Wittmann continued down into town, Dyas prepared to sneak up behind the Tiger and engage it in its vulnerable rear. Meanwhile Wittmann, having dealt with the RHQ Troop tanks, moved on to destroy the other RHQ Troop vehicles.

Stand A5: The Action with B Squadron

DIRECTIONS: At this stage it is better to drive south-west down the main road into Villers-Bocage, to the small market square between the very new Place de Maréchal Leclerc and the Place Jeanne d'Arc at the far end of town. There are public lavatories here and the tourist office, providing information on local amenities, town guides and so on. Leave your car and walk back up the main road, locating from the sketch-map and the photographs both here and in the history section (both the pre-war French postcards and the wartime German photographs), the approximate positions of the knocked-out vehicles.

THE ACTION: This is very difficult because all the buildings are new, but one can get the 'feel' of the Tiger's almost majestic progress as it dealt with each of the British armoured fighting vehicles it encountered. However, its journey through the town would not last much longer. Soon after destroying the two 5th RHA OP tanks, Wittmann was engaged by Sergeant Lockwood's Firefly, the leading vehicle of 2nd Troop, B Squadron, 4th CLY. Lockwood's tank had just entered the town, and so it was still some distance further down the street, probably at the eastern edge of Place Jeanne d'Arc. Both fired, but neither hit their target, the armour-piercing rounds striking nearby buildings instead.

Villers-Bocage, looking north-east up the main street (Rue Pasteur – D675). The Place Jeanne d'Arc is just to the right on the corner of the D675, with the D67 to Caumont-l'Éventé coming in from the left. This is roughly where B Squadron, 4th CLY, had reached when A Squadron was at Point 213. *(Author)*

However, being engaged by a 17-pounder rather than the far less powerful 75-mm of the Cromwell must have unsettled Wittmann, because he chose to withdraw, realising that he was meeting a stronger British force than he had so far encountered. Sufficiently obscured from the Firefly by the smoke and dust, the Tiger did a neutral turn and moved off in the direction of Point 213, gun to the front. Blocking his route of course was Pat Dyas' Cromwell, creeping along and hoping for a shot at the Tiger's rear end. Instead Dyas found himself staring down an 88-mm gun barrel. Although he did manage to fire twice, his rounds merely bounced off the Tiger's thick frontal armour. Wittmann then replied in kind, brewing up Dyas' tank with just one shot and literally blasting him out of the turret.

Unknown to Wittmann more trouble awaited him. As he was passing the blazing Stuarts near the Tilly-sur-Seulles turning, he was engaged by one of the 6-pounder anti-tank guns of A Company's anti-tank platoon, commanded by Sergeant Bray, which had somehow got into action. It hit the Tiger's driving sprocket and running gear, putting the tank out of action mechanically. Wittmann therefore had to abandon it. He decided

Captain Pat Dyas of RHQ, 4th CLY, who tried to stalk Wittmann's Tiger, but ended up being blown out of his tank. Fortunately he was able to recover sufficiently to get back to B Squadron and was then sent to the regimental aid post for treatment. *(Author's collection)*

not to destroy his tank, however, as it might well be recoverable later by the highly efficient company fitters. Instead he engaged all the British vehicles nearby, forcing everyone to keep their heads down. Then, taking what weapons they could with them, he and his crew baled out.

In the short time that had elapsed since the battle began, the British casualties had been considerable. A Squadron had lost three Cromwells and a Firefly; A Company, nine half-tracks, four carriers and two 6-pounder guns; RHQ Troop and Reconnaissance Troop, four Cromwells, three Stuarts, one scout car and one carrier; and 5th RHA, one Sherman OP and one Cromwell OP.

All of these apart from two of A Squadron's Cromwells had been knocked out by Wittmann in his Tiger, a formidable tally. But rather than get things out of perspective it should be remembered that none of the British vehicles stood much chance against such a powerful adversary, apart from the Firefly, and it only in firepower not in protection.

Stand A6: Château d'Orbois

DIRECTIONS: Wittmann and his crew then made their way to Panzer Lehr Division headquarters at Château d'Orbois, some 6 km to the north. One German account says that Wittmann and his crew walked via St-Louet-sur-Seulles and Feuguerolles-sur-Seulles, so by driving along the D33 to Château d'Orbois you are probably following the route they took.

THE SITE: This is where GenLt Bayerlein (the Panzer Lehr Division commander) had his tactical headquarters, a location which reinforces how vulnerable the British force was, so far behind the front line and so close to these crack German troops. It also helps to explain how worried the Germans were to know that British armour was so close to their rear.

The village of Orbois on the D33. Panzer Lehr Division had its headquarters in the château to which Wittmann and his crew made their way when his tank was knocked out. *(Author)*

Generalleutnant Fritz Bayerlein (second from left), the brilliant commander of Panzer Lehr Division, is seen here talking to I SS Panzer Corps commander *SS-Obergruppenführer* Sepp Dietrich (in greatcoat). *(Helmut Ritgen)*

Stand A7: Villy-Bocage

DIRECTIONS: Retrace your route to Feuguerolles-sur-Seulles and then turn left (east) along the D92, then south at the crossroads near Point 111 after 1.8 km, through le Buquet and towards Villy-Bocage some 2 km to the south. Just before the village look for the obvious water tower (possibly a folly for the nearby château) to the west of the road. Stop there and get out of your car. It provides an excellent vantage-point over the countryside all around, especially towards Villers-Bocage.

The site of the old water tower or folly to the north-west of Villy-Bocage gives an excellent view over towards Villers-Bocage and the area which was vulnerable to the Desert Rats' 'right hook'. *(Author)*

THIS IS THE END OF THE TOUR: Join the D6 at Villy-Bocage and continue into Villers-Bocage to end the tour or, to go back to Point 213 to go straight on with Tour B and the next phase of the battle, on leaving Villy-Bocage take the next left onto the D217c. Since Tour B takes up the action exactly where Tour A ends, there is no reason not to combine them into one, though you may wish to take a break in Villers-Bocage in between, perhaps for some shopping or a visit to one of the cafés or bars in the main street. If possible look also at the model in the town hall, which shows the town before it was flattened by the RAF, and perhaps meet Monsieur Henri Marie, the local historian.

The Jérusalem War Cemetery is the smallest Commonwealth War Cemetery in Normandy, with just 47 Commonwealth graves and one Czech. *(Author)*

Alternatively, you could return to Bayeux to enjoy some of the non-military sights or go on down to the fascinating Suisse Normande district to the south. On the way back to Bayeux you may also wish to visit the Jérusalem War Cemetery (48 burials). It can be found on the right-hand side of the D6 at the bottom of an uphill stretch about 2 km north of Bucéels.

TOUR B

VILLERS-BOCAGE: 1030 HOURS ONWARDS

OBJECTIVE: A tour covering the British defence of Villers-Bocage, the subsequent withdrawal to the Island Position and the actions there.

DURATION: The distance covered is only a few kilometres but it would be sensible to allow 1–2 hours in the town and additional time to orientate yourself in the Island Position.

APPROACH TO BATTLE: At Point 213, a number of events had now taken place and the British force was in a state of some confusion. A Squadron, 4th CLY's survivors comprised the crews of just seven Cromwells and two Fireflies. There was also the commanding officer's scout car and a 5th RHA Cromwell OP, which was attached to A Squadron. About a dozen 1st Rifle Brigade soldiers, plus a fair number of their officers (who had come up for the orders group) were sheltering in the ditches and hedges, their remaining undamaged vehicle strength being just three half-tracks and two scout cars.

4th CLY's commanding officer (Lt-Col Lord Cranley) and A Company's commander (Major Wright) conferred and decided to try to hold Point 213 until reinforcements from 131st Infantry Brigade arrived to take over. Some reorganisation took place, the tanks trying to move into positions from where they could provide all-round covering fire for the remaining infantry. However, they had not yet eliminated the Tigers on their southern flank and at least two more Cromwells were knocked out in exchanges of fire.

Knocked-out half-tracks of A Company, 1st Rifle Brigade, viewed from the west, looking up what was then the RN175 in the direction of Point 213. *(Bundesarchiv 101/494/3376/22a)*

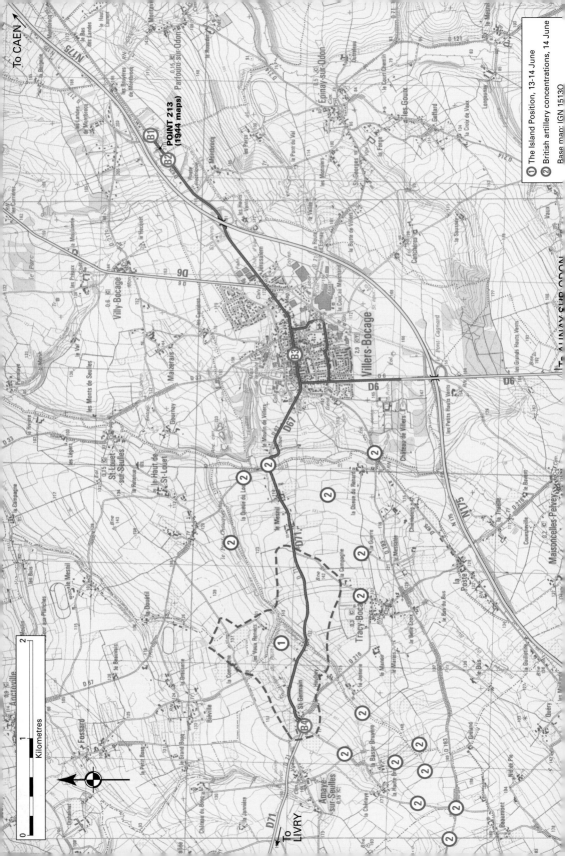

To CAEN

POINT 213
(1944 maps)

Parfouru-sur-Odon

Epinay-sur-Odon

Villy-Bocage

Villers-Bocage

Château de Villers

St-Louet-sur-Seulles

Tracy-Bocage

Maisoncelles-Pelvey

St-Germain

LIVRY

Amayé-sur-Seulles

Beaumont

Anctoville

① The Island Position, 13–14 June

② British artillery concentrations, 14 June

Base map: IGN 1513O

0   1   2
Kilometres

Stand B1: Point 213

THE ACTION: Meanwhile, 131st Infantry Brigade was still a long way away, only just entering the far western end of the town, and instead the next arrivals at Point 213 were men of 4th Light Company, 101st Heavy SS Panzer Battalion.

It is difficult to imagine the depth of the trauma which the British advance guard had suffered. The drive to Villers-Bocage that morning had been virtually trouble free and the reception they had received in the town had further lulled them into a false sense of security. The CO was probably the one person worried as he knew exactly how far they were behind enemy lines. However, he was being spurred on by his brigade commander. Then, out of the blue, they had been hit by point-blank fire from an unknown number of the most fearsome tanks on the battlefield – the dreaded Tiger, whose 'bite' was far worse than its 'bark', especially in the hands of an expert like Wittmann. Next, just as they had begun to organise some sort of defence around Point 213, unexpectedly more enemies had arrived – not more tanks, perhaps, but just as lethal to dismounted and totally disorientated infantry and tank crews – well equipped panzer-grenadiers with numerous automatic weapons. The German infantrymen soon began rounding up the British tank crews and infantry, winkling them out from their hiding places in the ditches and hedgerows, ready to march them off into captivity.

One of the Englishmen, however, was determined not to be captured and had a hair-raising adventure as a result. This was Captain Christopher Milner, second-in-command of A Company, 1st Rifle Brigade.

Milner had positioned himself covering the lane running north-east from Point 213:

'I was behind a small cottage. It was along this track that a peasant woman walked up to us, was detained as a possible spy, but after an hour or so, she slipped away. Was she a spy? Not long after, a Sharpshooters tank, edging forward around the bend along my lane, was hit and the wounded crew baled out having suffered the driver killed. They seemed to be pinned down so I crawled along the road and helped them to get back to the comparative safety of the cottage. I then lay on watch again... Suddenly there was a rumble of tanks from the east and as I darted round to the front of the cottage I was astonished to find that the tank shooting seemed to have ended and that some officers in black berets were standing about talking to one or two of our officers in the middle of the road.'

Milner started out to join them then 'froze' as he realised they were German tank crews!

This is the lane down which Christopher Milner 'escaped' at the start of his epic journey to safety. He would eventually walk almost in a circle and have to cross the road again in order to reach the British lines. *(Author)*

'I immediately turned and didn't run back where I'd come from but ducked into a little garden to the left and ran up inside the hedge in the direction of the enemy, not of our own people in Villers-Bocage. I went through a little gate beyond the garden still just inside the hedge with one of the German officers running along the road parallel to me shouting "Englishman surrender! Englishman surrender!" Fortunately he stopped after about fifty yards and talked to another officer who'd just arrived from the German side in a Volkswagen... At this stage I decided it was about time I died a hero's death and so I stood up and levelled my Sten gun at the two of them, at pretty well point blank range over the top of the hedge, took careful aim and pressed the trigger. But of course, like so many Sten guns, it decided not to work and just had the effect of sobering me up!'

Captain Christopher Milner MC of 1st Rifle Brigade. *(Merlin Milner)*

Milner sensibly decided that instead of drawing further attention to himself, he would try to escape, so he crept away. This involved passing near the knocked-out Cromwell whose crew he had helped earlier, crawling on his belly around the outside of a field, almost running into a troop of German guns whose crews were busily digging in, and having countless other near escapes – even having to dodge smoke shells which British gunners had fired, presumably to try to help the advance guard withdraw, but of course by then it was far too late.

Milner continues:

'Anyway the shells landed and it was difficult not to cough an awful lot, they gradually gave up and all was peaceful. It was a nice fine afternoon and I suppose I slept a bit. The only snag was that I was incredibly hungry and not a little thirsty… at last it began to get dark and I started to crawl slowly towards the main road again, that is to say towards the south side of the field. My plan was to wait until all was quiet, dash across the main road, over the intervening field to the parallel track… then turn back in a westerly direction towards Villers-Bocage and try to take a course which would bring me round the south side of the town.'

Milner waited until about midnight, when everything was quiet, sprinted across the road, dived into the hedge and made his way gingerly towards the town. After many more adventures he managed to reach British lines safely:

View on past Point 213 from whence Möbius and his company would have appeared. *(Author)*

'So that was my battle of Villers-Bocage, not very glorious I'm afraid and yet of any twenty-four hours of my life I can think of none which I can recall so clearly as I can those hours, which photographed themselves in my mind so that now, telling the story God knows thirty years later, I can see every yard of the route which I followed and every episode as clearly as if it happened last year.'

Source: Account given to the author in 1974 by Major Milner.

Stand B2: The German capture of Point 213

DIRECTIONS: One can roughly follow Captain Milner's escape route from the road, but there is little point trying to do so exactly as the new N175 has effectively cut off the track he mentions, so merely note the end of the lane where he started (*see photo on page 146*).

THE ACTION: The panzer soldiers that Milner saw at Point 213 were probably members of SS-Captain Rolf Möbius'

1st Company, 101st Heavy SS Panzer Battalion, who arrived about 1300 hours.

They were later joined by Wittmann, who had arrived from Château d'Orbois in a borrowed *Schwimmwagen*. No doubt he briefed Möbius very carefully on what to expect in Villers-Bocage but it is difficult to find any hard evidence that Wittmann himself actually led the new company in the second assault, as is claimed in some accounts.

However, some histories do aver that Wittmann's Tiger was in fact only slightly damaged during the first attack and that he returned to Point 213 at that stage to replenish fuel and ammunition, before leading the second assault, possibly in a borrowed Tiger from Möbius' company, and was then knocked out by an anti-tank gun as already described. Logically this is suspect for three reasons. First, why should the Germans say that Wittmann visited Panzer Lehr Division's headquarters at Château d'Orbois after the first battle if he did not do so until much later on – and he most certainly did visit Château d'Orbois that morning? Second, would a competent, experienced SS captain like Möbius defer to an officer of lower rank, however expert, and let him lead the attack? Third, Wittmann made a recording for a German propaganda radio broadcast on the evening of 13 June in which he graphically described the events of the first attack, ending in his tank being disabled and his subsequent visit to Panzer Lehr Division's headquarters. However, he then dismissed the second attack on Villers-Bocage in five words: 'Subsequent counter-attack destroyed the enemy.' Therefore, it sounds far more likely that he did not actually take part in the second assault, but that the Nazi propaganda organisation put its 'spin' into the official account so as to make Wittmann into even more of a hero, which was totally unnecessary after all the success that he had achieved already that day.

A good overall view of the chaos that was A Squadron, 4th CLY, up at Point 213, as German troops collect anything of use from the knocked-out vehicles. This view was taken looking back down the main road towards Villers-Bocage. (*Bundesarchiv 101/738/275/49*)

Other German reinforcements were also on their way, as *Major* Helmut Ritgen of Panzer Lehr Division later recalled:

'Before 1100 hours the author received orders to advance to the area north of Villers with every available panzer – about 15 – in order to prevent the feared strike in the division rear. The division general staff officer, *Major* Kauffmann, gathered all available soldiers from his staffs and other units in order to cover towards the south. All elements, especially the supply columns, were warned to avoid Villers-Bocage... Driving along the road from Juvigny, the author received instructions directly from General Bayerlein in Villy-Bocage. I was ordered to advance along the road to the west, block all exits from the town at positions north of the stream, in order to prevent an attack on the division rear. When the lead panzer reached the road to Anctoville north-west of the town, it was destroyed by a concealed anti-tank gun and burst into flames. We had run into the British all-round defence west of Villers.'

Source: Helmut Ritgen, *Memoirs of a Panzer Lehr Officer*, p. 47.

Stand B3: Villers-Bocage town centre

DIRECTIONS: Leave Point 213, drive through the town to the western end and take the D6 road due south towards Château de Villers. The town now stretches far further south than it used to, so instead of having to go cross-country take one of the roads to the old station (*Anc. gare* on the IGN map), locate it, then find your way back to the centre of town and park again.

Lieutenant Bill Cotton (left, in fur collared German flying jacket and wearing an Iron Cross!) poses with the rest of his crew after the battle. For his bravery he was awarded an immediate Military Cross. *(IWM B5682)*

Battle chaos around the *mairie* (town hall) in the centre of Villers-Bocage gives a graphic impression of the ferocity of the fight in which Lieutenant Cotton's troop of B Squadron, 4th CLY, knocked out a Tiger (*right*), one of Möbius' 1st Company tanks, and a Panzer IV belonging to Panzer Lehr Division. The two tanks are seen here side by side amongst the rubble, facing towards Place Jeanne d'Arc. (*Bundesarchiv 101/494/3376/89*)

The town hall has been moved into the newly-built Place de Maréchal Leclerc, while the square where it stood has been re-built and is so altered as to make it impossible to follow what happened on the ground, so please look at the aerial photograph on page 75 instead. Remember that Lieutenant Cotton, his tanks and their supporting infantry anti-tank gun were waiting in ambush for the Germans to arrive.

THE ACTION: Back in Villers-Bocage, at the western end of the town, Major Aird of B Squadron had assumed command of what was left of the 4th CLY group. Being unable to make any progress up the main street, he sent Lieutenant Bill Cotton, commander of 4th Troop, to try to find another way forwards.

Cotton's troop comprised two normal Cromwells, plus one (Cotton's) equipped with the close support 95-mm howitzer (useless in a tank-versus-tank battle) and a Firefly (commanded by Sergeant Bobby Bramall). Cotton drove south down the D6, until he was fired on from the vicinity of Château de Villers. He then turned east and motored across country to the railway. As the railway embankment blocked any further eastwards movement, he now turned north and found a route up to the town hall square. Here Cotton established a troop ambush position.

Villers-Bocage, looking south-west from the Place de Maréchal Leclerc. This large square on both sides of the main road contains the town hall (on the southern side), where the model of wartime Villers-Bocage is located. (Author)

Meanwhile 1st/7th Queen's (Lt-Col Gordon) had begun arriving at the western end of the town, while German infantry were infiltrating into the eastern end. House-to-house fighting took place all over Villers-Bocage, both sides getting very spread out and fragmented. After some while, Gordon decided to pull his forces back into a tighter defensive position, with A, C and D Companies holding the perimeter, together with their anti-tank guns, while B Company was battalion reserve.

At the town square Lieutenant Cotton had dismounted from his close support Cromwell and parked it out of sight, having decided to control the fire of his other three tanks on foot. Engines were switched off and everyone listened for the unmistakable track noises that would herald the approach of the enemy. As well as Cotton's tanks, there was a Queen's 6-pounder anti-tank gun nearby. Some of the Panzer Lehr Division's Panzer IVs had already begun to infiltrate into the town, as had Möbius' Tigers. Two of the leading Panzer IVs were knocked out by the Queen's anti-tank gun, so the Tigers took their place. As well as the Tigers and the Panzer Lehr Division Panzer IVs, more vehicles belonging to 2nd Panzer Division were approaching from the south, so the German forces in the area were increasing to an even more formidable size.

The leading Tiger motored slowly and carefully into the square and was immediately engaged by Sergeant Bramall's Firefly at point-blank range. Unfortunately, the first round he fired passed clean over the top of the Tiger, because the gunner could not use his sights properly, as the range of engagement was too short. Nevertheless, the Tiger was then engaged by the Queen's 6-pounder anti-tank gun and knocked out. Despite the fact that the Germans must have been expecting an ambush, they had clearly been taken off guard – so, first blood to the British.

Villers-Bocage, this time looking south-west towards the Place Jeanne d'Arc and the western entrance into town. *(Author)*

Villers-Bocage, still on the main street looking north-east, just where the D71 joins it from the south. *(Author)*

The rest of the German attackers now knew where the ambush was located, so they began to try to outflank it. One group of three Tigers reached the Place du Marché, then separated. One of them proceeded via the back gardens of the houses towards the industrial area at the southern edge of town. However, when it had almost reached its goal it was knocked out by a Queen's 6-pounder gun hidden in an alleyway. A second tank of this group moved along Rue Emile Samson, but it was also knocked out – this time by a PIAT. The third Tiger was moving along Rue St-Germain, making towards the town war memorial (located near the town hall), when it was also knocked out by a PIAT.

There next followed a remarkable tank-versus-tank duel, between Sergeant Bramall's Firefly and another Tiger. Bramall had spotted the German tank stationary, hiding around the corner in the adjoining road (Rue Pasteur), waiting to get a shot at any unsuspecting British tank. He quickly realised that the only way he would get a clear shot at this Tiger was by pulling his tank back a few metres until he could line up the gun through two adjacent windows in the corner building. He did so, then had to make his final corrections by looking through the breech and along the barrel (shades of Clint Eastwood in the film *Kelly's Heroes*!). He then loaded the 17-pounder and fired two rounds in quick succession, hitting the German tank on its mantlet, unfortunately where its thickest armour was located. However, having been engaged by Bramall, the Tiger first pulled back, then tried to rush past the ambush. The troop corporal, Corporal Horne, was ready, however, and waited until the Tiger was past, then shot it up its rear, where its armour was thinnest. The Tiger rolled on down the road for about 30 metres, then came to a halt and did not move again. The 'window engagement' was later immortalised by a drawing in the *Illustrated London News*.

Sergeant Bramall would follow this success by knocking out a further Panzer IV. Later, during a lull in the fighting, he and Lieutenant Cotton went around the knocked-out German tanks in the vicinity carrying a bundle of blankets and a jerrican of petrol, and set fire to them, so they could not be recovered. Cotton would be awarded the Military Cross and Bramall the Military Medal for their bravery and skill in the defence of Villers-Bocage.

The second battle had now lasted for over two hours, the main activity at one time shifting to A Company's position, which was

Rear view of one of the wrecked Tigers, from which it is clear that it was set on fire; note the smoke and scorch marks around the open escape port on the rear of the turret. *(Bundesarchiv 01/494/3376/11a)*

This is how the remarkable tank-versus-tank engagement was depicted in the *Illustrated London News*. Although the British tank looks more like a Crusader than a Sherman Firefly, the engagement of the German Tiger 'through the windows' is shown very dramatically by the accomplished war artist Bryan de Grineau. *(Illustrated London News)*

around the railway station. However, as the afternoon progressed, the men of 1st/7th Queen's were forced out of the station area and into a tighter perimeter further west. Gaps began appearing in the British line through which the Germans were able to infiltrate. By 1700–1800 hours German infantry were getting even closer to the remaining 4th CLY tanks, while 1st/7th Queen's battalion headquarters had become pinned down. The road into Villers-Bocage from the west was also under heavy German artillery and mortar fire.

Stand B4: The Island Position

DIRECTIONS: Leave Villers-Bocage at the north-western corner of the town, following the D67 for a few hundred metres before bearing left onto the D71. Pass through le Mesnil, which marked the eastern edge of the Island Position and exit the hamlet towards the west. Drive slowly, providing it is safe to do so, and note the high ground immediately to the left (south) of the road, which was defended on 14 June by D and A Companies, 1st/7th Queen's Regiment, supported by elements of 5th RTR. The slightly lower ground to the north of the road, sloping down towards the stream of the Ruisseau du Coudray, was held by the 1st/7th Queen's C and B Companies. Continue towards the next village, St-Germain, crossing the Ruisseau du Coudray as you do so. On 14 June 1944, the orchards to the south of the road in this area were occupied by 22nd Armoured Brigade's Tactical Headquarters, protected by troops from 1st Rifle Brigade, and C Company, 1st/5th Queen's. On reaching the western perimeter of the British position at St-Germain, park where it is safe to do so. If you wish to inspect the Island Position more closely, you can walk back along the road towards le Mesnil (2 km away); use the detailed map on page 81 to help you locate the various British positions. However, please respect private property at all times, and do not walk along hedgerows or into orchards unless there is an obvious right of way, or you have permission from the owner(s).

THE ACTION: The situation was now deteriorating so rapidly that Brigadier Hinde decided to pull back out of Villers-Bocage and to form a 'brigade box' just to the east of Amaye-sur-Seulles. In fact it was not just 22nd Armoured Brigade that was to be withdrawn, as battalions of 131st Infantry Brigade were also involved, so it is perhaps more accurately described as being a 'divisional box'. Part of the division (1st RTR and 1st/6th Queen's), however, had the special task of re-opening the D71–D115 route by which the advance had originally been made (it had since been cut by the Germans) and then protecting it, so that the other British units would be able to pull out safely and make their way back to Livry if necessary.

Amayé-sur-Seulles was occupied by a British patrol during the fighting for the Island Position. *(Author)*

The elements of 22nd Armoured and 131st Infantry Brigades were squashed into a very tight perimeter only some 1,800 metres wide by not much more than 1,300 metres deep from north to south. This meant that every wood and orchard was congested with transport, tanks and guns, presenting perfect targets for German aircraft or artillery. Remember that the British force was still a long way within enemy territory and therefore extremely vulnerable. However, they were able to call for a massive amount of artillery support, both from Second (British) Army and First US Army to their immediate west, and had plentiful RAF ground-attack support, too. Unfortunately, however, the 'Island Position' was overlooked on three sides, though changes in the landscape mean that it is hard now to get a proper idea of how difficult the immediate countryside was. The elements of 1st/7th Queen's, for example, were facing towards Villers-Bocage with their forward lines based in a sunken ditch and with fields of fire of barely

100 metres – difficult to imagine today looking over the more open terrain.

The first night on the Island Position, 13/14 June, passed quietly enough, but at about 1100 hours on the morning of 14 June there was a determined German attack, only broken up after a violent small-arms battle in which there were heavy casualties on both sides. Although at one point the forward positions of 1st/7th Queen's were overrun, the assault was finally defeated and the position restored. However, at about 1900 hours the Germans put in a more powerful two-pronged attack, this time on the south and north-east sides of the box. One estimate was that a whole brigade of panzergrenadiers supported by more than 30 tanks was involved. After fierce fighting the attack was crushed (*see pp. 84–5 for details*).

Unfortunately, despite the fact that all were now confident that the position could be held, it was clear that 50th Infantry Division would be unable to break through in its sector (around Tilly-sur-Seulles) to relieve 7th Armoured Division. The corps commander felt, therefore, that he must straighten his line and had accordingly decided to pull 7th Armoured Division back to a line through Livry, which was achieved successfully, as described on pages 86–7.

The view back to Villers-Bocage from the D67 road. *(Author)*

THIS IS THE END OF THE TOUR: What chaos the remarkable Michael Wittmann had caused. Granted, he had a massively superior tank in every respect to those of his opponents. He would have been able to stand off at range and knock out his enemy without putting himself into immediate danger. Instead, however, he chose to go not just into the lion's den but right down its throat. In doing so he showed courage of the very highest order and fully deserved the award of the Swords to his Knight's Cross and promotion to *SS-Hauptsturmführer*.

TOUR C

THE BATTLES FOR LINGÈVRES AND LES VERRIÈRES

OBJECTIVE: A tour examining 9th DLI's attack on the village of Lingèvres and the near-simultaneous action by 6th DLI against les Verrières on 14 June.

DURATION: You should allow half a day for this tour if you want to cover both villages properly and visit all areas. The distance covered is not great – not more than 10 km at most (from the centre of Lingèvres) – but it is worthwhile trying to get into all the little lanes, trying to take up the actual tank fire positions and so on, so as to get a real feel for the two battles.

APPROACH TO BATTLE: The British plan for the Tilly-sur-Seulles area was for a two-phase operation, which was to begin with attacks to take the high ground immediately west of Hottot-les-Bagues and would involve 6th DLI and 9th DLI of 151st Infantry Brigade, 50th Infantry Division. On the right 9th DLI was tasked with capturing the village of Lingèvres, and on the left 6th DLI was to capture the adjoining hamlet of les Verrières and then go on to take Hottot-les-Bagues. The operation would start on 14 June. Each battalion was supported by a squadron of 4th/7th Dragoon Guards – A Squadron on the right and B Squadron on the left. 4th/7th Dragoon Guards was equipped with M4 Sherman medium tanks, a proportion of which were Sherman Fireflies. To the brigade's right flank 231st Infantry Brigade would carry out a similar assault on la Senaudière.

Stand C1: Point 89

DIRECTIONS: Drive south from Bayeux on the D6 to Tilly-sur-Seulles then west along the D13 into Lingèvres. Stop on the side of the road opposite the church and war memorial. Having acquainted yourself with the general layout, take the right fork (D33a) just past the church winding to the north-west, then north, and make your way up through the farmland to the obvious road/track junction (Point 89) about a kilometre north of the village. This is Stand C1. Stop here and turn round so that you are looking down the slope into the village. You can see some of the houses quite clearly and, dependent upon the time of year, also see across to les Verrières (the 'les' does not appear on the wartime maps) on your left front.

THE ACTION: You are now just in front of the British forward defence lines (FDLs) of 14 June 1944. The Germans held the village and the wooded areas to its north. They had had time to prepare their positions, digging deep slit trenches so as to avoid the worst of the Allied air attacks and artillery fire and had cut the standing corn about 60 metres short of the woods to form a killing zone.

The two DLI battalion commanders had been called to 151st Infantry Brigade headquarters on the afternoon of 13 June and received orders to take the villages early the next day. Lt-Col Wood, commanding officer 9th DLI, had said to the brigadier, 'Brigadier, you know if we do this we shall have a tremendous number of casualties. We ought to do this attack at night and we ought to have some time for reconnaissance.' The brigadier agreed, but explained that this was a vital battle and that no time could be lost in capturing the villages because of the pressing need to continue the breakout from the beachhead.

Later, in his orders to his company commanders, Wood explained that a reconnaissance in force would take place that

les Anges

90
①

89
C1
②

les Grands Longuets

③
84
C5
④

89

Stèle
ⓐ
les Verrières

82.5
77

91

D 33a

D 187
D187

le Landey

Bérolles
⑤   ⑥

82

les Feuillets

D13
C4

Éc.
C2   C3

84

D 1

90
C6
92
D13

0,5   C

Lingèvres   le Tour
d'Hiver
Bnie
96

Lieu Meslier
94

les Flagues

101

Lieu Dufresne
Corillon

101

90

le Parc de la

les Pourprains   le Mesnil

0.5   1
Kilometres

① C and D Companies, 9th DLI,
elements A Squadron, 4th/7th RDG

② A and B Companies, 9th DLI,
elements A Squadron, 4th/7th RDG

③ D and A Companies, 6th DLI,
elements B Squadron, 4th/7th RDG

④ C and B Companies, 6th DLI,
elements B Squadron, 4th/7th RDG

⑤ D Company, 6th DLI

⑥ B Company, 6th DLI

ⓐ Monument to 4th/7th RDG

Base map: IGN 1512OT

Looking south down the D33a at Lingèvres from no-man's-land to the north. This is the road astride which 9th DLI, supported by A Squadron, 4th/7th Dragoon Guards, advanced against heavy German fire. The standing corn had been cut close to the wooded area just in front of the village, but was still growing further north. (*Author*)

evening in daylight, to try to discover the strength of the enemy and their locations. This was undertaken by B Company, supported by the carrier platoon and an artillery forward observation officer. The Germans allowed them to get into the killing zone and then subjected them to withering fire, forcing a withdrawal with considerable casualties – a taste of things to come. Clearly the Germans were in strength, probably seasoned troops (in fact they were from Panzer Lehr Division), and capable of holding their fire until it would be most effective. Two tanks were also seen in support, one being knocked out by a 102nd Anti-Tank Regiment (Northumberland Hussars) M10 self-propelled anti-tank gun from the battalion positions.

Wood had opted for a simple plan of attack. The battalion and its tank support would cross the start line – about a kilometre behind the FDLs – at 1015 hours on 14 June. The centre line would be the line of the road and the advance would be in box formation with A and B Companies on the left of the road and C and D on the right (*see tour map*). The commanding officer was behind A Company and Major John Mogg, his second-in-command, behind C Company. About 15 minutes before the

attack started, Typhoon aircraft would drop bombs and blast the woods with rockets. There would also be considerable artillery support from three self-propelled field regiments and the whole of 5th Army Group Royal Artillery (three field regiments, three medium regiments, a heavy regiment and an American artillery battalion). Infantry/tank co-operation was simple and well practised, the infantry using yellow air recognition panels tied to the ends of rifles and waggled in the air, then pointed in the direction of concealed German positions. 6th DLI's attack was timed to start at 1130 hours, so that it too could have the full benefit of a similar artillery barrage and air strikes.

The attack began on time, the barrage opened up and the Typhoons did their stuff.

One observer commented:

'We were treated to a front seat at a very accurate and sustained 25-pounder barrage and the woods literally jumped and danced in front of our eyes and not three hundred yards away. The Typhoons, each one, did one dive and each one released two bombs and ten rockets, straddled and plastered that wood. Surely nothing could live in that now.'

Source: Quoted in David Rissik, *The DLI at War.*

How wrong he would prove to be.

The companies moved off at H-Hour, in straight lines, two platoons of each company in front followed by the third platoon. The men went forward at a steady walk, their rifles across the chests, bayonets glinting in the sun, rather reminiscent of a First World War attack. On the flanks were the tanks of A Squadron, 4th/7th Dragoon Guards (commanded by Major Jackie d'Avigdor-Goldsmid). As they got nearer to the village, the barrage lifted from the front positions and moved on into the village. As it did so, the Germans came to life and began to put down heavy, accurate fire, from well-sited machine-gun positions, while two tanks opened up and were engaged by A Squadron's Shermans. It was soon clear that A Company on the left was suffering severely as it tried to cross the killing zone and get to grips with the defenders. All of A Company's officers were now casualties, including the two forward observation officers, the vital link to the artillery. B Company took over but was also soon decimated.

On the right flank things were going better, so Lt-Col Wood called his second-in-command, Major John Mogg, on the radio and ordered him to push ahead, saying that he would try to extricate the two left flank companies and swing them round to reinforce C and D Companies. That was the last transmission which Wood would make, because a mortar bomb hit his carrier and he was killed. Major Mogg immediately took over command.

A stretcher-bearer of 9th DLI attending to German wounded near Lingèvres after the initial battle to capture the key village. *(IWM B5525)*

Major Mogg recalled later:

'We went through the corn and the Geordies are never very tall guys and the corn that year was extremely high. We marched the whole way across the corn, with the barrage still going on and suddenly you saw the odd Geordie dropping in the corn. You couldn't quite make this out, where it was coming from, when in fact it was machine-gun fire from the edge of the woods and quite a lot of Geordies were dropping in the corn all the way along. However we advanced... we got into the woods... C Company had lost quite a number of chaps and I had to pass D Company through. We got into the village... '

Stand C2: Lingèvres War Memorial

DIRECTIONS: Go back to the village. The large farm you pass on the right hand side just before the village proper became Mogg's battalion headquarters later. Go on past the farm and stop in the car park just before the D33a joins the main road. Walk to the crossroads near the war memorial and church. There is also a memorial to 50th Division here.

Bérolles Farm, which became both Mogg's headquarters and the regimental aid post, once 9th DLI had captured the village. *(Author)*

THE ACTION: In fact 9th DLI reached the village just before noon, then began the difficult task of winkling out the remaining Germans from the houses and gardens. The tanks had stayed with the infantry all the way into the village, their support proving invaluable, especially during the house-to-house fighting. They would continue to protect the infantry against the sudden appearance of German tanks once the Geordies were in full possession of the village. The battalion had taken quite severe casualties. D Company was still fairly strong, but C was only at about single platoon strength, whilst the remnants of A and B were yet to join them.

Mogg, now acting commanding officer, held a quick orders group and disposed his forces:

'I ordered "D" Coy to occupy the East and SE edge of the village... facing towards Tilly and "C" Coy of one platoon to look after the approaches from the South. I made a DF [defensive fire] plan with my gunner, [Major] Ken Swann of 86 Fd Regt.

I ordered the support weapons to move forward, putting the carriers to guard the Western approach and set up my Bn. [Battalion] HQ in the area of the bridge over the stream just North of the village and on the Bn. axis. I sited the five remaining A. Tk. guns singly, facing down the road approaches. This was a fatal mistake as in the first counter-attack four of the five were knocked out by advancing tanks coming down the road. It taught me never to site A. Tk. guns to fire frontally but always to engage tanks from the flank.'

Source: Taken from a briefing given by the then General Sir John Mogg for a Staff College Battlefield Tour in the 1970s.

It was now that the 4th/7th Dragoon Guards tanks really came into their own, against the predominantly tank threat. The German tanks were, however, no mean opponents, being Panthers, perhaps the best medium tanks of the war. Their high velocity, long barrelled 75-mm L/70 guns, able to penetrate 140 mm of armour plate at 1,000 metres, were far superior to the low velocity 75-mm weapons on standard Shermans. The Sherman's 75-mm gun could not penetrate the Panther's front

Wilfred Harris

Sergeant Wilfred Harris was born in Walsall in 1911, so like Wittmann he was in his early thirties by the time of D-Day. Harris was a pre-war Regular in the 4th/7th Royal Dragoon Guards, earning the nickname 'Spit' – short for 'Spit and Polish' – because of his immaculate dress. Released from the colours in 1935, he joined the Motor Transport Troop, A Squadron, when recalled in 1939. However, after surviving Dunkirk, he volunteered to train as a tank commander. By 1944 he was an experienced troop sergeant, who looked after his men and was well liked, admired and trusted by his crew. His actions at Lingèvres gained him the Distinguished Conduct Medal and promotion to squadron quartermaster-sergeant. He survived the war and later served in the War Department Police. Wilfred Harris died in 1988. The Lingèvres action has been immortalised in a painting by David Shepherd that now hangs in the Royal Dragoon Guards Officers' Mess.

HRH The Duchess of Kent, Colonel-in-Chief of 4th/7th Royal Dragoon Guards, seen here at York in 1987 talking to former Squadron Quartermaster-Sergeant Harris DCM (with walking stick) and two members of his crew – Jack 'Nibby' Garside (driver) and Richard Eagles (loader/operator). *(Mrs Val Nevitt via Author)*

BATTLEFIELD TOURS

armour even at point-blank range, although it could go through the side armour provided the Sherman could get close enough. As at Villers-Bocage, however, the 'ace up the sleeve' was the 17-pounder gun on the Sherman Firefly. 4th Troop of A Squadron was to be the close support troop in Lingèvres and it had the usual complement of three 75-mm Shermans and just one Firefly. The Firefly was commanded by Sergeant Wilf Harris, with Trooper Ian Mackillop as his gunner. It did not originally belong to the troop, having been ordered to join them in the village as the original 4th Troop Firefly had, as Harris put it, 'gone astray'. This attachment was vital because at least two Panthers had been seen to the east of the village. The troop leader, Lieutenant Alastair Morrison, disposed his tanks as follows: Morrison's own tank was at the base of the church tower in the centre of the village; Harris' Firefly covered the road east out of the village towards Tilly-sur-Seulles; Sergeant Roberts covered the road from les Verrières; Corporal Johnson, in the final 75-mm Sherman, watched the road south (to Longraye).

Sergeant Harris takes up the story:

'On joining the troop I dismounted from my tank and went over to speak to my new troop leader and find out the form. He gave me the direction of the two Panthers and other information and asked me to take up a position not far from him. I found a very nice defensive position and put my tank there.'

In addition to Lieutenant Morrison's troop, there was another Sherman in the village – the observation post tank belonging to the forward observation officer, Major Swann. Like all OP Shermans it had a wooden gun on the outside of the mantlet, so that the entire turret could be taken up by additional radio sets and other equipment needed to control the artillery fire. Although this meant it was useless as a gun tank, Swann proved invaluable in providing close fire support during the almost continual German counter-attacks.

Stand C3: Harris' First Position

DIRECTIONS: Walk to the eastern end of the village to where the D187 forks off to les Verrières. You are now approximately in Sergeant Harris' first position.

The eastern end of Lingèvres, looking east along the D13 in the direction from which the first German tanks appeared. Harris must have been slightly further back behind the crest of the hill as he was unobserved by them. From here he destroyed two Panthers moving across his front from south to north. *(Author)*

THE ACTION: Harris recalled, 'I must have been there about ten minutes when it was reported that two Panthers were advancing towards us. I couldn't see them at first, but I didn't

The eastern end of Lingèvres village, looking westwards along the D13 towards Harris' position. The cover from fire and from view that he would have achieved from the hill is now apparent. *(Author)*

have long to wait.' In fact there were three tanks approaching, two Panthers led by a 'decoy' Sherman, moving across from south to north, the Sherman suddenly peeling off further to the north.

> 'Keeping my eyes open I picked up the two Panthers about 1200 yards away, creeping down a hedge. I was confident they couldn't see me, so I held my fire and let them get closer. By this time my gunner (Ian Mackillop) had the leading tank well in his sights and when it was about 400 yards away I opened up and to my amazement the first shot sent it into a mass of flames and with the second shot we did the same to the second Panther.'

After this success, Harris sensibly moved to another fire position where he was able to shelter behind a cottage and thus get some cover. Retaliatory fire was now aimed at him by the second Panther, which had only been disabled and still presented a real threat. Something had to be done to silence it, so Mogg decided to lead a tank-hunting party out personally, to knock it out with a PIAT. He took with him a sergeant and a private from nearby D Company and they crept stealthily forward until they were only some 15 metres from the enemy vehicle. 'Right,' said Mogg, 'when I say fire, fire!' To his chagrin he then discovered that neither of his companions knew how to fire a PIAT. Fortunately, however, he did and he then succeeded in knocking out the Panther.

This was not the only tank-hunting that had been in progress. 9th DLI's anti-tank platoon commander (Lieutenant Ken Whittaker) had earlier spotted a Panther in a barn further down the Longraye road (the D187 to the south) and had asked Major d'Avigdor-Goldsmid, A Squadron's commander who had recently arrived by the church, to help. The two of them first carried out a 'foot recce', creeping past the knocked-out anti-tank guns and confirming that the Panther was still in the barn. Unfortunately the subsequent tank-hunting party failed to knock out the Panther (due to their PIAT misfiring) and it drove off southwards unscathed.

Soon afterwards, while trying to move into a better fire position, Corporal Johnson's Sherman guarding the southern road was knocked-out by an armour-piercing round and all his crew except one were killed or wounded.

The most serious German attack was about to take place and would again by thwarted by Sergeant Harris and his Firefly. There had been a short lull in the fighting, then it was reported that German tanks had been seen on the western side of the village on the Balleroy road (D13 west). Major d'Avigdor-Goldsmid ordered Captain John Stirling, who was providing flank protection some half a kilometre to the north-west, to investigate. This Stirling did; making the most of his Sherman's superior mobility, he managed to get into a flanking fire position and knocked out one of the Panthers.

Stand C4: Harris' Second Position

DIRECTIONS: Walk back past the car park. Just a few metres beyond the end of the car park is an obvious culvert, then a junction to the left which leads onto the D13 on the western side of the culvert. From here through gaps in the trees and bushes you can still just about see the bridge over the culvert on the D13 road, despite the fact that the trees are now taller than in 1944. Walk along the little joining road to the D13. From here it is possible to fix the positions where two Panthers were about to be destroyed (*see overleaf*).

The western end of Lingèvres village, showing the lane down which Harris moved in order to take up his new position watching the western approaches to the village. (*Author*)

Although this view of the D13 is partly obscured, it is still possible to see part of the stonework of the bridge over the culvert. *(Author)*

THE ACTION: The effect of Stirling's attack, as a XXX Corps report put it, was like putting:

> '... a ferret in a rabbit hole. Within the space of two minutes, three Panther tanks moved down the road West to East and as they passed, Sgt Harris shot them.'

It was spectacular shooting. Harris knocked out the first tank before it entered the village. The second one bypassed its companion and was also hit. Even so it managed to reach the centre of the village, but remained there with its sprocket blown off, the crew having baled out. The third Panther was also hit and destroyed – making the score six to 4th/7th Dragoon Guards, with Harris having accounted for five of them, for the loss of just one Sherman.

Harris described how he saw the engagement:

'Immediately I was in position I got my gunner to lay his guns on a certain spot along the road so that when I hit the first tank the second would be in my view. During this time the four Panthers were halted on the road about 1500 yards short of the village. I could hear the squadron leader giving orders to another troop to knock out the rear tank and draw the other three forwards into the village where we were all waiting. This worked just as he

Then: The western end of the village of Lingèvres, still with the two Panthers in the places where Harris knocked them both out. The bridge over the culvert is also plainly visible. *(IWM B5784)*

Now: The same view along the D13. *(Author)*

wanted, the rear tank was KOed and the others started to race for the village. In doing so they had to pass the spot on which my gun was laid. I was ready and as soon as the leading tank got there I fired; it brewed up immediately. The second tank overtook the leader but then fell victim to my second shot. I immediately trained onto the third tank and brewed that one up as well. The village remained ours and I was pleased with my gunner who had knocked out five Panthers with five shots.'

Source: Account written by Squadron Quartermaster-Sergeant Harris, supplied to the author by Mrs Val Nevitt.

This action concluded this phase of the fighting. Harris and his crew, in particular his gunner Trooper Mackillop, deserve our admiration for the way in which they fought their tank. Remember that they were not in a 57-ton Tiger, but rather a 34-ton 'Ronson Lighter', whose armour could easily be penetrated by its opponents at extreme ranges, and then was virtually guaranteed to burn. It takes a remarkable degree of courage to get the job done in such circumstances.

Stand C5: Point 84

DIRECTIONS: From Lingèvres, take the left hand fork, the D187, at the eastern end of the village off the D13. Continue past les Feuillets and les Verrières, taking the left hand fork at the small stele (a monument to 4th/7th Dragoon Guards) up north into the fields. Stop at about Point 84 in the open farmland and look back to the south.

THE SITE: You are now once again approximately on the British FDLs and if you look to the right you should be able to pick up the position of Stand C1 in front of Lingèvres. Of course it will depend upon the time of year as to how much you can see; the roofs of the buildings at les Verrières should be visible, however.

APPROACH TO BATTLE: The British plan to capture the high ground dominating Tilly-sur-Seulles also involved 6th DLI, supported by B Squadron, 4th/7th Dragoon Guards. After a day of hectic action on 13 June, 6th DLI had been withdrawn

The 4th/7th Dragoon Guards memorial near les Verrières, lists the following who gave their lives: 2nd Lt C. Robertson, Sgt C. Fry MM, Sgt J. Watson, L-Cpl D. Hickey and Troopers J. Busbridge, W. Dunn, R. Edmed, D. Thomasson and J. Wood. *(Author)*

through 2nd Battalion, The South Wales Borderers', positions and bivouacked for the night at Folliot, some 3 km north of les Verrières between the D33a and D178 roads. Its mission for the following day was to capture les Verrières and Hottot-les-Bagues,

Les Verrières from the north. Most of these buildings were probably standing during the war and would have been visible as the men of 6th DLI approached the main German trench line. *(Author)*

which lay a further 3 km to the south. As already explained, the air and artillery support would be as for the 9th DLI attack, with a slightly later H-Hour.

THE ACTION: 6th DLI moved out astride the road from Folliot to les Verrières, with C and D Companies leading, B and A Companies following up in reserve, and B Squadron, 4th/7th Dragoon Guards in support. To begin with the attack went well until they were immediately north of their first objective. Here, as in the 9th DLI attack, the attackers entered a cleared killing zone and the whole German line – based on a large ditch on the southern edge of the field now only some 150 metres away – opened up with devastating rifle and machine-gun fire, causing many casualties. The attack was held up whilst more artillery blasted these positions, but even this failed to deal with the opposition. It was later found that the Germans had their machine guns mounted on tripods and could fire them remotely, the machine-gunners being well dug in to the side of the ditch and thus protected from all but a direct hit.

> **Private Ernest Harvey of 6th DLI later recalled:**
> 'We were all going into the attack and we were going across this cornfield. We got about 20–25 yards into the cornfield when Jerry opened up with Spandaus. Well [there was] a small groove in the ground where, fortunately, I got into it. I got down. The men were getting mown down left, right and centre. In fact the company was being slaughtered, it's as simple as that. As those were going down more were coming up and these were getting knocked down. The cry then was, "Mother! Mother!" I know it's a funny thing but everybody was crying for their mothers. Eventually two tanks came up behind us. This was after a long while and all the corn had been completely mown down by the Spandaus – we couldn't move. If you moved you got shot. You had to stay down and I remember, two tanks came up and they blasted this hedge... Eventually we took the position but the point was that nearly all the men had gone... You'd think they'd expected us coming... I only thought that happened in WWI. I never thought it would have happened in 1944.'
> *Source:* Quoted in Harry Moses, *The Faithful Sixth*.

BATTLEFIELD TOURS

German prisoners, captured at Lingèvres and les Verrières by 6th and 9th DLI, are marched past a damaged cottage in Bernières, 2 km to the north-west of the two villages. *(IWM B5532)*

The reserve companies pushed through and took over the attack. Although they also suffered many casualties, after some five hours of heavy fighting, the position was taken at around 1600 hours. 6th DLI then paused to reorganise along the line of the ditch, turning some of the captured machine guns onto the retreating Germans. Then, while A and D Companies remained in the ditch, B and C went forward to clear the village and try to reach the main road (the D13).

Stand C6: B Company's Advance

DIRECTIONS: Drive back past les Verrières, pausing to look at the buildings and at the 4th/7th Dragoon Guards monument. Continue down the D187 to join the D13 and then turn left, stopping at the junction with the small road up to les Verrières. Look north and you can see the route taken by B Company as it tried to reach the main road.

THE ACTION: B Company got through les Verrières without any trouble, crossed the Ruisseau du Pont St-Esprit, then paused on the left of the track to allow D Company to come up on the right. The commander of one of the supporting Shermans, Lieutenant Jenkins, saw a German tank at the crossroads with the main road, covering the track astride which the Durhams were advancing. Its fire quickly pinned down D Company. B Company had managed to get forward to within some 200 metres of the main road when it came under intense fire from both the tank's machine gun and other well-camouflaged machine-gun positions.

Les Verrières from the south. The gaggle of buildings proved to be a difficult nut to crack as is evidenced by the heavy casualties sustained. *(Author)*

On the left, one section of one platoon managed to reach the road. However, it also came under heavy fire, four men being killed and two wounded. The four survivors would remain hidden in the roadside ditch for the next two days, before, amazingly, being picked up by their company when it eventually reached the road.

This was as far as the assault would manage to get, all companies then being withdrawn to the line of the track just north of les Verrières where they dug in for the night. Patrols were sent out the following day and found that the Germans had withdrawn, so the battalion moved forwards to the disputed crossroads and dug in. That would be the limit of their advance that day.

Men of the DLI digging slit trenches by the roadside to resist German counter-attacks. The photograph, taken on 16 June, gives a graphic impression of the height of the *bocage* hedgerows. *(IWM B5644)*

THIS IS THE END OF THE TOUR: The battle for les Verrières had been extremely costly. 6th DLI had suffered 23 killed and 65 wounded, including three officers, and 15 were missing, bringing the battalion's total casualties since landing on D-Day to 192 killed, wounded and missing. B Squadron, 4th/7th Dragoon Guards, had lost five tanks in the les Verrières battle, with five crewmen killed, eight wounded and four missing.

There are a number of memorials and war cemeteries near Lingèvres and les Verrières which you may wish to visit. The *Tilly-sur-Seulles War Cemetery* (990 Commonwealth and 232 German burials) is located just off the D13 on the south side about 1 km west from the centre of the town.

If you continue south from Tilly on the D6 and then turn west on the D9 the *Hottot-les-Bagues War Cemetery* (1,137 burials, of all nationalities) is on the right after about 600 metres. You can then continue into Hottot-les-Bagues where, in the Place du Dorset Regiment, there is a memorial to 231st Infantry Brigade.

Museum of the Battle of Tilly

Musée de la Bataille de Tilly, Chapelle Nôtre Dame du Val, 14250
Tilly-sur-Seulles; tel: +33 (0)1 31 80 80 26. Open May–Sept, closed Oct–Apr.
Entrance fee.

The *Battle of Tilly-sur-Seulles Museum* is located in a twelfth-century chapel (Chapelle Nôtre-Dame-du-Val) in the town. It tells the story of the violent battles that took place around Tilly between XXX Corps and the Germans. It was captured, lost and recaptured some 23 times before finally being liberated. The village was completely rebuilt after the war. Outside the museum is a memorial plaque to the 24th Lancers.

The Battle of Tilly-sur-Seulles Museum is housed in a twelfth century chapel in the town. *(Author)*

To reach the *Fontenay-le-Pesnel War Cemetery* (519 burials) continue east from Tilly on the D13 then join the D139 south-eastward. About 1 km out of Fontenay there is a memorial to 49th (West Riding) Infantry Division on the right-hand side. Opposite it is a track leading to the cemetery.

PART FOUR

ON YOUR
RETURN

FURTHER RESEARCH

All the books listed in the bibliography are well worth reading in order to provide further information on this intriguing story. For overall background on the battles, however, probably the best small book is Belfield & Essame's *The Battle for Normandy*, whilst Carlo D'Este's brilliant *Decision in Normandy* and Alistair Horne's *The Lonely Leader*, which he wrote with Viscount David Montgomery, are also strongly recommended.

The battle of Villers-Bocage and the part played by Michael Wittmann have long been the subject of many books, some of which unfortunately seek to glorify the *Waffen-SS*. This has led to accounts of what was a remarkable action by a brave and highly competent tank commander and his crew being deliberately enhanced. This was initially done during the war by the Nazis for obvious propaganda purposes, but has unnecessarily led to myth being treated as fact. Therefore, it is not easy to find a full and fair account of this battle.

In my opinion, the person who clearly knows more about what happened at Villers-Bocage on 13 June 1944 than anyone else is the local Villers-Bocage historian, Monsieur Henri Marie, who has studied it in minute detail and written about it at length, his books being published by Editions Heimdal of Bayeux. This first-class French publisher does market books in the UK via Chris Lloyd of Poole (Chris Lloyd Sales & Marketing Services, Stanley House, 3 Fleets Lane, Poole, Dorset BH15 3AJ, tel: 01202 785712, email: <chrlloyd@globalnet.co.uk>). Some of the Heimdal books are bilingual. One would also find it difficult to better, for a balanced, detailed study of the Villers-Bocage battle, Daniel Taylor's *Villers-Bocage Through the Lens of the German War Photographer*, which contains many photographs of the immediate aftermath of the battle, together with a more constructive and unbiased commentary than most other books. After The Battle publishers have also produced Eric Lefevre's *Panzers in Normandy*, which deals with many other tank battles in Normandy as well as Villers-Bocage.

Above: Fontenay-le-Pesnel Cemetery contains 519 graves, mainly British, with four Canadians and 59 Germans buried there; the identities of 26 of the dead remain unknown. *(Author)*

Page 183: In the fighting for Lingèvres, Major Mogg quickly found out that this was definitely not the way to site anti-tank guns. This particular 6-pounder anti-tank gun actually belonged to 7th Green Howards, but it was in the Lingèvres area and photographed on 16 June 1944. *(IWM B5642)*

Of course as most of these authors and publishers swiftly discovered, the Bundesarchiv in Koblenz has undoubtedly got the pick of the post-battle photographs, as it has the entire series taken by the official Nazi photographers. The Imperial War Museum photographic collection contains a smaller selection, but useful to fill in the gaps. This is valuable because of course Villers-Bocage was so effectively flattened that virtually nothing remains of the old market town.

On the other hand, the battles around Tilly-sur-Seulles are well covered both in the histories listed below and in the Imperial War Museum Photographic Department. Lingèvres, although rebuilt, fortunately remains much as it was before, so it is considerably easier to follow the battles there than at Villers-Bocage.

FURTHER SOURCES OF RESEARCH

While there is nothing to beat a visit to the actual area, it is not difficult to approach the sources of the basic material you will need, such as the UK National Archives, to obtain wartime maps (to supplement the modern ones), photographs, war diaries and so on. In this connection a visit to the Tank Museum at Bovington, Dorset, is strongly recommended. Not only does it hold copies of all the war diaries of the Royal Armoured Corps regiments concerned, but it also has examples of all the tanks which took part in the battles. The Bayeux Memorial Museum has already been recommended. Also worthwhile are the French Tank Museum at Saumur and the German equivalent in Munster, both of which have first class collections of armoured fighting vehicles. Good hunting!

Useful Addresses

UK National Archives, Public Record Office, Kew, Richmond, Surrey TW9 4DU; tel: 020 8876 3444; email: <enquiry@nationalarchives.gov.uk>; web: <www.nationalarchives.gov.uk>.

Imperial War Museum, Lambeth Road, London SE1 6HZ; tel: 020 7416 5320; email: <mail@iwm.org.uk>; web: <www.iwm.org.uk>.

British Library, 96 Euston Road, London NW1 2DB; tel: 020 7412 7676; <email: reader-services-enquiries@bl.uk>.

University of Keele Air Photo Library, Keele University, Keele, Staffordshire ST5 5BG; tel/fax: 01782 583395; web: <evidenceincamera.co.uk>.

Tank Museum, Bovington, Dorset BH20 6JG; tel: 01929 405096; web: <www.tankmuseum.co.uk>.

Musée des Blindes, 4940 Saumur; tel: +33 (0)2 41 51 02 45; web: <www.musee-des-blindes.asso.fr>.

Das Deutsche Panzermuseum, Hans Krüger Strasse 33, 29633 Munster; tel: +49 (0)5192 2552; web: <munster.de/pzm>.

BOOKS

Basley, Olivier, *Tilly-sur-Seulles: Un Village au Milieu de l'Historie*, Musée de Tilly-sur-Seulles, 2000

Belfield, Eversley, & Essame, H., *The Battle for Normandy*, Severn House Publishers, 1965

Bernage, Georges, *The Panzers and the Battle of Normandy*, Editions Heimdal, 2000

Bradley, Omar, *A Soldier's Story*, Henry Holt, 1951

Clay, Ewart W., *The Path of the 50th: The Story of the 50th (Northumbrian) Division in the Second World War*, Gale & Polden, 1950

Delaforce, Patrick, *Churchill's Desert Rats: From Normandy to Berlin with the 7th Armoured Division*, Sutton Publishing, 2003

D'Este, Carlo, *Decision in Normandy*, Collins, 1983

DIREN (Direction Regionale de l'Environnement de Basse Normandie), *Gardens of Remembrance*, Editions Orep, 1999

Dunphie, Christopher, & Johnson, Garry, *Gold Beach: Inland from King – June 1944*, Pen and Sword Books, 1999

Eisenhower, Gen Dwight D., *Crusade in Europe*, Heinemann, 1948

Foster, R.C.G., *History of The Queen's Royal Regiment: Volume VIII 1924–1948*, Gale & Polden, 1953

Graham, Andrew, *Sharpshooters at War*, The Sharpshooters Regimental Association, 1964

Hamilton, Nigel, *Master of the Battlefield: Monty's War Years 1942–1944*, McGraw Hill, 1983

Horne, Alistair, with Montgomery, David *The Lonely Leader*, Macmillan, 1994

Isby, David C. (ed.), *Fighting in Normandy: The German Army from D-Day to Villers-Bocage*, Greenhill Books, 2001

Lefevre, Eric, *Panzers in Normandy: Then and Now*, After The Battle, 1983

Lindsay, Martin, & Johnston, M.E., *History of the 7th Armoured Division June 1943 – July 1945*, first published by BAOR in 1945, reprinted in 2001 by DP & G for the Tank Museum

Marie, Henri; Bernage, Georges; Benamou, Jean-Pierre; & Mari, Laurent, *Villers-Bocage: Champ de Bataille le Combat des Tigres*, Editions Heimdal, 1993

Marie, Henri, *Villers-Bocage*, Editions Heimdal, 2003 (both in English and French)

Mollo, Boris, *The Sharpshooters 1900–2000*, Kent and Sharpshooters Yeomanry Trust, 2000

Montgomery, Bernard L., *Normandy to the Baltic*, BAOR, 1946

Moses, Harry, *The Faithful Sixth: History of the 6th Battalion, The Durham Light Infantry*, County Durham Books

Moses, Harry, *The Gateshead Gurkhas: A History of the 9th Battalion, The Durham Light Infantry 1859–1967*

Newton, Cecil, *A Trooper's Tale*, Cecil Newton, 2000

Ritgen, Helmut, *The Western Front 1944: Memoirs of a Panzer Lehr Officer*, J.J. Fedorowicz, 1995

Taylor, Daniel, *Villers-Bocage Through the Lens of the German War Photographer*, After The Battle, 1999

Verney, G.L., *The Desert Rats: The History of the 7th Armoured Division 1938 to 1945*, Hutchinson, 1954. Reprinted 2002 by Greenhill Books

OFFICIAL/UNOFFICIAL PAPERS USED FOR REFERENCE

Immediate Report No 4, issued by Main HQ XXX Corps 17 June 1944 (Source: PRO WO 171/336)

Report on Operations of 7th Armoured Division in Normandy 6–30 June 1944. Issued by Main HQ 7th Armoured Division 14 July 1944; containing a separate report by commander 22nd Armoured Brigade on operations 6–15 June. (Source: Papers of the late Maj-Gen G.T.A. Armitage, thanks to Alec Armitage, Esq)

The Sharpshooter – Newsletter of the Sharpshooters Yeomanry Association (Extracts published here by kind permission)

Correspondence between Maj-Gen Erskine and J.H. Yindrich of 7 August 1952, presumably during the preparation of a book that was never published – now held by the Tank Museum Library. (Extracts published by kind permission)

Five members of 1st Rifle Brigade are buried in the small churchyard of St-Exupère, just off the Eisenhower roundabout on the Bayeux ring road. *(Author)*

INDEX

Page numbers in *italics* denote an illustration.